The Concentration C
The True Story of a Belgia

AUSTIN MACAULEY PUBLISHERS™
LONDON • CAMBRIDGE • NEW YORK • SHARJAH

VERA MERTENS

The Concentration Camp:

The True Story of a Belgian Teenager

First published in Dutch in October 2017
First publication of the English translation 2019
Copyright © 2017 Vera Mertens
Cover photo Madrolly / Getty Images
Author's photo © Ilse Ervynck
Editorial support Luc de Rooy
Translation © Eileen Stevens
Editor Linden Lawson
Book design Studio De la Rúa

Copyright © Vera Mertens (2019)

A CIP catalogue record for this title is available from the British
Library.

ISBN 9781528915434 (Paperback)
ISBN 9781528915441 (Hardback)
ISBN 9781528961233 (ePub e-book)

www.austinmacauley.com

Austin Macauley Publishers Ltd
25 Canada Square
Canary Wharf
London
E14 5LQ

Lest we forget!

I walk along the graves where Belgian, English and Canadian war heroes lie in rest. The unbearable silence nearly drives me away, but I sit down at the Second World War monument and look at the long rows of white crosses. The red glow on the horizon takes my thoughts to the Midway Atoll and the rolling waters of the Pacific Ocean, which contain the bodies of so many American soldiers who fought for freedom, democracy and prosperity. The screeching of gulls brings me back to the cemetery. As darkness stretches over the graves, I leave with the thought: 'It was on Midway that the fighting spirit of the Japanese was broken. That was a turning point in the war. After that, the Japanese were defeated on Guadalcanal. If the Americans had lost on Midway, then the United States wouldn't have had enough resources to protect the West Coast, and the landing on Normandy might never have taken place. Then I would never have been able to write this book, *The Concentration Camp: The True Story of a Belgian Teenager.*'

Sources:
In writing this book I drew on what I had learned first-hand from my father about the war years 1940–45, and augmented that with additional information passed on to me by my mother, her sister-in-law Elise, family and friends. In addition, I consulted sources including:

– The Belgian Federal Public Service Social Security, Directorate-General for War Victims. My father's personal file.

– The official Internet site of the United States Navy: Chief of Naval Operations CNO Admiral John M. Richardson. The honors he received included the Vice Admiral Stockdale Award as commander of the *USS Honolulu*.

– *Oorlogskranten*, 1940–45 (war newspapers from 1940–45): an independent publication that has been created in association with the Belgian CegSoma – Study Centre War and Society, with special support from the Royal Library of Belgium.

– A. van der Heyden: *Oorlogskroniek der stad Aalst: De tweede maal!* (*War Chronicle of the City of Aalst, the Second Time*), *Vijf jaren lief en leed in de stad van Dirk Martens (1940–45)*, (publisher: Van der Heyden Aalst, 1976).

– https://nl.wikipedia.org/Lijst_van_gebeurtenissen_tijdens_de_ Tweede_Wereldoorlog:_1940 up to and including 1945.

The Concentration Camp:
The True Story of a Belgian Teenager

PRECEDING EVENTS

It was chilly, and the mist had spread over the Flemish fields. As night was falling, Pierre lay in front of the crackling fire with a book, enjoying the warmth. He was interested in politics, just like his father and his grandfather. He was especially interested Adolf Hitler, the leader of the National Socialist German Workers' Party, or NSDAP. Pierre had read about how the German Reich Chancellor had used a cunning maneuver to sideline parliament; how he'd withdrawn from the League of Nations, rearmed Germany and occupied the Rhineland. Pierre went to his room with the book under his arm. There he read that the German leader had found an ally in Italy's fascist ruler Mussolini and that Austria had voluntarily joined the Third Reich.

Even though his eyes were getting heavy, he swapped the book for the newspaper beside his bed and read that Germany had forcibly annexed Czechoslovakia. He looked at the photo of Hitler, who was addressing the crowd. The German people seemed very enthusiastic! He got out of bed, went downstairs, sat beside his father and asked: 'How has Adolf Hitler got so many citizens behind him?'

'That's a long story,' answered Pa Florent. He tossed another log on the fire and said: 'Hitler joined the German Workers' Party in September 1919; he had a seat on the governing board and gave public speeches because he had a talent for that. When the party's founders left the scene, Adolf Hitler was seen as the new leader. He changed the name of the party to the National Socialist German Workers' Party, now commonly known as the Nazi Party, because that dovetailed more closely with his ideology. In 1921 Hitler established the 'Sturmabteilung', literally the Storm Division, or SA. He did this with Ernst Röhm, a former army captain who led the SA and supplied it with weapons from the army depot. In the beginning, the SA consisted primarily of thugs whose job it was to protect NSDAP members from the opposition during meetings. Ernst Röhm maintained an anti-capitalist policy, but Hitler didn't warm to that because he desperately needed the business world's financial support to implement his plans. In 1925, the 'Schutzstaffel' – meaning Protective Squad, and commonly known as the SS – was set up to protect the leadership of the NSDAP party. By 1933 the SA numbered some 400,000 members, while the German Army scarcely had 50,000 troops. In January of that same year, the Reich President, Paul von Hindenburg, reluctantly appointed the poorly educated Hitler as Reich Chancellor. The Reich President died shortly afterwards, and Hitler immediately added the powers of the President's office to his duties as Chancellor. There was an immediate protest, but Hitler quashed the resistance and banned all parties except the NSDAP. In 1934 the SA's members' magazine appeared. In it, a lot of attention was focused on Ernst Röhm, but Adolf Hitler hardly received a mention; for this Hitler wanted revenge. Röhm and the other influential people in the leadership of the SA were liquidated. With the help of the financial specialist Hjalmar Schacht, the Führer – as he now called himself – restored the German economy and reduced unemployment. Hitler censored the press, and this gave him free rein. He deceived the population to the point where the German people massively supported their leader, and he became enormously popular. But Hitler was a dictator: he didn't tolerate any dissent, and everyone had to subscribe to his ideas and obey him. He implemented social controls, and anyone who stood in his way had to be eliminated!'

'Adolf Hitler is a dangerous man!' Pierre concluded while petting the head of his dog, Markie. He went back to bed, quickly skimmed the article about the persecution of Jewish people and jotted down the details in his *cahier*. That's what he called his notebook, because they spoke French at home.

Just then, Pierre's sister Eveline – who was five years older – came home from her nightly escapades. Her messy hair and smudged make-up betrayed the fact that she hadn't been out walking on her own. She opened the door of his bedroom and said: 'Pierre, put that notebook away and go to sleep!'

Pierre used black ink to circle the official date of the commencement of the public persecution of Jews; then he turned out the light. When he woke up, the first thing he thought about was Adolf Hitler. At breakfast he brought up the persecution of the Jews, and, slurping his warm milk, asked his father: 'Why does Hitler hate the Jews?'

'Nobody knows. It most likely has something to do with his childhood. In his youth Hitler was a poor loser, a lowlife who wasn't popular with the bourgeoisie. He was thrown out of school when he was fourteen. Adolf wanted to go to art school, but wasn't talented enough, and wasn't admitted. He didn't have a diploma and couldn't find any work, so he did odd jobs to earn money. That's why Hitler hated everyone who had it better than him, especially wealthy Jews because they had well-paying jobs. The man was driven by hate, and when he came to power he set up a concentration camp in Dachau to detain the Jews and make them disappear from the face of the earth. Hitler opened other concentration camps soon afterwards. In fact, it's not just the Jews he despises, but homosexuals, gypsies and disabled people as well. In short, everyone who's different!'

Pierre reacted with disgust. The milk he'd been drinking lost its taste. He tossed his slice of bread to Markie, grabbed his coat from the chair and left for school. When he got home that evening, Gaston, a friend of his father's, was sitting at the table. He was a frequent guest. Pierre closely followed their discussion about the impending war.

1939

After a period of relative calm, ominous news once more started to emerge from Germany.

'Deutschland über alles!' Pierre read aloud from the newspaper, and added: 'The journalists write that Hitler wants to stir up the populace. He'll stop at nothing to achieve his goals.'

'Yes, the headlines speak for themselves,' replied his father.

Turmoil escalated. The situation became critical, and gas masks were distributed. In August 1939 the mobilization was quickly intensified. Those who were called up had to join a unit immediately. For many, the farewells were hard to bear.

That morning, Pierre and his friend Felix rode their bikes to the station. The two lads witnessed the heartbreaking scenes taking place between family members, acquaintances and friends. One woman waved goodbye to her husband and burst into tears. A little further ahead, a child pulled himself free from his mother's grasp and ran desperately after his father. The man wrapped his arms around the little fellow, covered him with kisses and brought him back to his mother. At the entrance to the station, a young woman sat crying on the curb, waving to her boyfriend. The sound of the chimes from the Belfort tower prompted Pierre to look at his watch. It was getting late. The boys hurried over to the city park, where the gang they belonged to were meeting. Together, they evaluated the threat of war, and the friends retold atrocious tales of battle in the fading light. Pierre, who lived nearby, left for home around ten o'clock that night. When he got there, his father was sitting by the fire with the notebook.

'Pierre, I read here in your notes that Hitler and Stalin stunned the rest of the world when they signed a non-aggression pact in Moscow. Do you know why everyone thought that was so extraordinary?'

'Yes, because it was so unusual for the extreme left and the extreme right to reach a compromise! There was still an enormous ideological gulf between the two regimes. They were most likely up to something.'

Pa Florent gave Pierre an admiring look. He saw in his son the spitting image of his own father.

Some weeks later, Pierre thumbed through the newspapers that had been saved for him and circled the fact that Great Britain and France had simultaneously declared war on Germany after the German Army invaded Poland. The Russian military overpowered the eastern section of Poland. He noted that the two armies managed to stay out of each other's way, thanks to the sinister pact agreed by Stalin and Hitler. Before he went to bed, he read one more article about the Canadian province of Newfoundland, which had joined the Allies.

1940

The winter that followed hit them hard: temperatures dropped to well below freezing. It remained quiet in the Belgian city of Aalst, but in Pierre's house on the Parklaan they talked about the approaching war almost every night.

On a Wednesday afternoon in March, Pierre and Felix walked through the center of town: the atmosphere was tense. The first ration books were being handed out. There was increasing anxiety among the population; people hoarded massive amounts of provisions and stocked up on firewood. In the city park, rare trees had even been chopped down and reduced to kindling. The neighborhood police had their hands full with those types of petty crime.

As a precaution, many of Aalst's valuable works of art were removed from public buildings and stored safely. Civic workers lent a helping hand as Pierre and Felix looked on. The Générale Bank on the main street took in most of the valuables for safekeeping; paintings and precious objects were put away in the churches and monasteries as well.

Pierre and Felix had agreed to meet up with their friends, and bicycled to the park. They talked with their buddies Smekens, Eelbode, de Moor and Hazard about the threat of war, which had been somewhat averted the previous autumn following the Munich conference between Chamberlain, Daladier, Hitler and Mussolini.

'Public unrest is growing again,' said Pierre.

'Everyone is on high alert. The army is waiting and ready,' said Felix, his finger raised for emphasis.

'Are we prepared to fight to protect our independence and to preserve our freedom?' demanded Pierre.

'We are prepared!' the friends answered in unison.

Full of anticipation, the gathering broke up.

In April, Pierre read that the German Army had attacked Denmark and Norway. He jotted this down in his notebook and discussed the article with his father. Pa Florent warned: 'The war is still very close and can't be avoided, even though King Leopold III has chosen to pursue an independent policy by breaking with the Franco-Belgian Military Accord of 1920.' He convinced his son that – as a civilian in service to the country and its people – his duty was to stand wholeheartedly behind the monarch. Pierre ran his hands through his blond hair, yawned, and went to bed.

Felix rang the doorbell around seven o'clock in the morning. Pierre had just got out of bed; he splashed some water on his face, combed his hair, grabbed his jacket from the chair and shut the door behind him. Then they rode to school together on their bikes.

They paused for a moment when they got to the school gate. Hardly anyone had shown up. The boys decided to turn around and bike to the center of town. Civilians were waiting in long lines at the banks and post offices where they had deposited their money. Pierre suspected that these people wanted to withdraw their savings. The boys looked up when they heard a rumble from above. There was an unusual amount of air traffic. A truck driver's shouting and cursing attracted their attention. The Belgian Army was requisitioning the man's vehicle. The soldiers were adamant, and they soon parked the truck alongside the many other confiscated vehicles in the public square. Bicycles were also being frantically seized. The boys walked among the heavily armed soldiers stationed in public buildings, warehouses, factories and storage sheds.

'In our neighborhood, a vacant house was requisitioned by the army,' Felix said as they peddled towards one of the bridges over the River Dender, which had been under military guard for some time. From a distance they could see the camouflage netting being removed from the machine guns and the anti-aircraft gun. The boys hung around near the bridge until it started to get dark. Pa Florent was waiting for Pierre at the door.

'This is serious! Every strategic location is being guarded,' Pierre said loudly to his father before he even got off his bicycle.

WAR: 1940–45

Pa Florent sat beside the radio. The howling sirens and the roar of the unending procession of military vehicles driving through the streets had kept him awake. He was startled by a brief bombardment and the shots from an anti-aircraft gun that followed. The children managed to sleep through the racket.

'The Germans have invaded Belgium,' said the radio announcer on Friday morning, 10 May 1940. Then interference disrupted the broadcast. Pa Florent shrunk back – his face lost all its color. He clenched his fists and looked exasperated. The horrors of the Great War came back to him like it was yesterday. He'd been part of the Grenadier Regiment and had recently been transferred to the 1st Rifles Regiment, when he got frostbite in his toes during a battle and contracted gangrene. Since then, he'd suffered terrible pain and regularly received injections of morphine. The illness was unstoppable: bit by bit, pieces of his limbs had to be amputated. Pa Florent used to love city life: his father had been an established figure in Aalst's political scene, and the family had frequently been invited to numerous social events. Pa Florent played the cello, and performed on a regular basis. He glanced at his maimed legs and realized that things would never be the same. He stared into space and suddenly his head filled with images of his late wife Joanne, who had died in 1936. For years, she had cared for him lovingly. Pa Florent had been left behind, bereft, with his five children. Since then, their governess Celina had taken on Joanne's tasks. Their previously cosmopolitan lifestyle had been replaced by an existence dominated by pain and grief.

The static from the radio shook Pa Florent awake. He pulled himself together and rang the bell to get the children out of bed.

'War's broken out!' he hollered from the bottom of the staircase.

Fourteen-year-old Pierre was the first to barrel down the stairs. He went to sit beside his father and wrote on the cover of his notebook: War, 10 May 1940. King Leopold III, Supreme Commander of the Belgian Army.

'That's right, isn't it?' he asked.

His father nodded. The infernal commotion from the bombardments reduced Pierre's two sisters and two brothers to tears. Celina sought cover in the cellar with the children. Once there, their younger brother Gustaaf had an asthma attack. The boy suffered from asthma and usually lodged with a family in Kessel-Lo, near the hospital where he received treatment, but just then he happened to be home. Gustaaf came back regularly to be with his family because that's how Pa Florent wanted things.

The asthma attack ceased as soon as the bombing stopped. Pierre wanted to slip outside behind his father's back. Celina tried to stop him.

'You're not my mother,' he shouted as he slammed the door behind him.

He ran down the street, but just as he disappeared around the corner dozens of German dive-bombers – known as 'Stukas' – appeared in the sky. Pierre sought cover. From his shelter, he could see how the aircraft hovered in the air to pinpoint their targets. Then they dived with a hellish wail and bombed the city. The attacks were impressive. Pierre couldn't move – he was frozen with fright. Pa Florent stood shouting from the front door while the heavy bombardment continued. It was useless – his son couldn't hear him above the racket. The bomb strikes were horrific. When the noise died away, he ran home. His father was furious. Pierre raced upstairs to escape his father's wrath.

'You're out of your mind! What if something had happened to you!' Pa Florent roared from the foot of the stairs.

Once his father had calmed down, Pierre came back downstairs.

'I had no way of knowing they were going to start bombing again,' he said.

Pa Florent sat glued to the radio with Pierre beside him. They listened to reports about the arrest of August Borms, who had been one of the most notorious collaborators during the Great War. Two other men had been detained as a precaution. One was Staf de Clercq of the Flemish National League, also called the VNV, an authoritarian party which collaborated officially with the Germans and wanted to secede from French-speaking Belgium and join the Netherlands. The other was Léon Degrell of the far-right Rexist Party. The broadcast was then broken up by interference.

The sirens stopped howling. The danger had passed. Shortly afterwards, Felix rang the doorbell.

'Pierre, want to go take a closer look at the damage?'

'Right now it's too dangerous in the city; the fire department will have their work cut out' warned Pa Florent.

The morphine Pa Florent took for the pain soon did its work, and he nodded off. Celina took advantage of the opportunity to steal yet another of his expensive cigars, and while she was smoking it she said: 'Pierre, you're not going out!'

He ignored her, because although his father had warned him of the dangers, he hadn't explicitly forbidden him from going out, and because Celina wasn't his mother. So the two boys headed for the city.

'Felix, did you know that King Leopold III – as Supreme Commander of the Armed Forces – has moved into Fort van Breendonk?'

'Yeah, I heard. My father also told me that the military are hard at work reinforcing and extending the lines of defense, and securing all the strategic locations.'

The boys arrived at the Zeeberg Bridge, where the planes had missed their target: the bomb they'd dropped had fallen on a nearby house and had cost many civilians their lives. Taking their bikes over the viaduct was not an option: the ramps leading up to it had been heavily damaged by the bombardments. Pierre and Felix watched silently as the emergency services pulled lifeless bodies from the wreckage: not just English soldiers, but ordinary citizens as well. They biked to the station via the inner city, which had been heavily hit. The damage to the station and the neighboring factories was indescribable, and the firemen and emergency workers were hard at work. Then the blast from an explosion blew the boys from their bicycles. The two crawled back up and cycled home. Pierre's father woke up the moment he arrived.

'Pa, the damage to the city is unbelievable!'

'Has the station been bombed?'

'Yeah, the station, the factories, the wharf, the paths leading up to the viaduct – everything's taken a beating.' But Pierre kept his mouth shut about having been blown off his bike by an explosion.

The following day, no bombers appeared above the city of Aalst. Celina stood looking out of the window as she tried to pick up what Pa Florent and Pierre were whispering. A few moments later, the lad attached his notebook to the luggage rack on the back of his bike and peddled off to the center of Aalst. Long rows of fleeing civilians, packed and ready to go, wound through the streets. Among the endless train of fleeing people he recognized one of his favorite classmates and asked: 'Where are you going?'

'We're on the run from all the violence. The German forces are on their way, and we're trying to reach the French border.'

'Be careful!' Pierre shouted above the din of the mob, as he rode away on his bike. Pierre arrived at the Madelon, a well-known local café and banquet hall, and parked his bike at the side. He went in and spoke with some men who were much older than he was. He was there on his father's behalf. He saw an empty chair next to Gaston, and sat down.

'Hitler's surprised everyone. German troops have attacked Belgium, the Netherlands and Luxembourg. We must resist these cowardly intruders who have invaded our country without warning, without a declaration of war or any ultimatum. England and France have already promised us their support. Columns of English military are driving through the streets as we speak,' said the meeting's chairman.

Suddenly Pierre left the meeting. He ran to his bike and looked quickly at the luggage rack. His face turned red, he balled his hand into a fist and angrily threw away the pen he'd been holding. There was no one around, except for a homeless person slumped against the wall along the footpath and a man in uniform.

'Have either of you by any chance seen someone near my bicycle?' Pierre asked.

The soldier shook his head and the vagrant didn't even look up. Pierre returned to the meeting.

Pa Florent's brother Jef rushed over to visit before noon. He lived in the center of town and had been running the family business on the main shopping street since their father's death. Pa Florent still owned a share of the business, but he worked as the head of customer service at the Belgian National Savings Bank. Uncle Jef had brought along some newspapers he'd been lucky enough to pick up in town. The brothers couldn't wait to start talking about the latest developments: Germany had invaded Belgium, the Netherlands and Luxembourg.

'What an outrage! Hitler wants more power in the world!' Pa Florent said. After that he talked about Churchill, who had replaced Chamberlain in the United Kingdom.

Just then, Pierre came into the living room. Pa Florent immediately noticed that something was wrong and asked: 'What's going on?'

Pierre ran up to his room. Uncle Jef followed him. The boy explained that his notebook, filled with all his observations, had been stolen. Jef gave his nephew some money to buy a new one. Pierre put it where he kept the rest of his savings: in some empty cigar boxes hidden in the secret double floor of his wardrobe. He went back to the living room and sat beside his father.

'I'd tied the *cahier* to my bicycle's luggage rack, and when I went to get it, it had disappeared!'

'Sacre bleu!' exclaimed Pa Florent, 'someone must have stolen it!'

Pierre was about to give his account of the meeting when Gaston rang the bell. Jef took his leave. Gaston and Pa Florent had been friends for years, and Gaston was a frequent visitor. While Celina poured the coffee, Gaston described what he'd learned at the meeting: 'The Belgian government hadn't gotten any advance warning of the attack. It was a surprise. The German ambassador waited until hours after the invasion to hand a memorandum to Prime Minister Spaak, saying that quelling the Belgian press was one of the reasons for the attack.'

Pa Florent took a sip of his piping-hot coffee and said: 'The Germans still remember their defeat during the Great War. The Nazi movement, under Hitler's leadership, wants revenge.'

They talked about Hitler for the rest of the night.

In the early morning, sirens suddenly began to wail. Celina fled with the children to the cellar, but Pa Florent remained sitting where he was. The deafening noise of the dropping bombs reduced him to tears. Pa Florent hated crying, so he got out his cello and began to play. Pierre pushed the cellar door open so the kids could listen to the music. It calmed them down. Someone rang the bell, pounding on the door and shouting like crazy.

'Florent, let me in! This violence has brought the city to its knees.'

Pa Florent couldn't hear a thing because he was still playing his cello, so Pierre came up from the cellar with his dog Markie at his heels. Pierre sent the dog back to the cellar and opened the door. Uncle Jef stumbled in, out of breath. Pa Florent stopped playing. In fits and starts, Jef managed to say: 'I was near the station when all hell broke loose. A heavy explosion was followed by a burst of flame that created an enormous cloud of smoke. One soldier said a train filled with petroleum had caught fire. The sea of flames grew into an inferno. It was awful!'

'The German ground forces are approaching Aalst. The surrounding municipalities are already taking a beating,' Pa Florent said as he sent Pierre back to the cellar, because the bombing hadn't let up. The brothers talked about how best to deal with the situation. All the while, the dignified house on the Parklaan was shaken to its foundations by the explosions.

In between the bombing runs, British and Belgian soldiers were working feverishly on the lines of defense. They blew up the bridges over the Dender and set fires to stop the Germans' advance. Once the bombing had stopped, the Germans erected temporary bridges over the Dender and their ground troops invaded Aalst. The heavy fighting caused large numbers of British, French and Belgian armed forces to retreat. After the invasion, chaos reigned. A few hours later Pierre heard the thud of soldiers marching. From his place in the cellar, he used his home-made periscope to see what was happening on the street.

'The Germans have got their hands on our soldiers,' he said furiously.

He raced up to his room, grabbed his collection of minerals from the cupboard, opened the window and loaded his catapult. Pierre aimed at the enemy. The small stones bounced off the Germans' helmets. The soldiers looked around, perplexed. Celina caught Pierre pelting them. She took away his catapult and threw it in the fire. Pierre was too late to rescue his weapon from the flames. 'Are you completely out of your mind?!' he shouted at Celina.

On the streets, the Belgian and English soldiers were replaced by Germans. The occupiers immediately issued a set of mandatory regulations: parties, gatherings and meetings were forbidden. Weapons had to be turned in. A closing time was imposed upon pubs, and there was a compulsory blackout in the evenings and at night. Those and countless other rules were printed on posters and hung up in the large market square and around the city. One of the Germans was on a ladder hanging up a poster when Pierre's little brother Franske raced into the lane in his father's wheelchair. Franske liked to drive it like a sports car, but this time there were some serious consequences. He ran into the German's ladder, and the soldier came crashing to the ground. Franske ran. He didn't dare look back, and he hid the wheelchair, continuing on foot. When he got home he didn't mention the incident to his father, who was listening to news about how the Netherlands had capitulated after heavy bombing. Franske confided in Pierre, who waited until dark and then went to retrieve the wheelchair.

'God help us!' Pa Florent exclaimed on the evening of 28 May 1940, when he heard on the radio that King Leopold III had capitulated and the Belgian government had fled to France. Germany had seized power.

'Pa, didn't you tell me that my duty as a civilian – serving the country and its people – was to stand steadfastly behind the monarch?'

'You know, Pierre, the King has never been able to get along with the government. He was always bothered by how quickly ministers succeeded one another, and how they let themselves be led by non-constitutional organizations like political parties and trade unions.'

Pa Florent frowned when he heard reports on the radio that Italy had declared war on France and Britain.

The city grew calmer and the schools were reopened. Jef paid a visit to his brother Florent, and he started talking right away about Staf de Clercq, the leader of the VNV, who had met with the leadership of the German occupation authorities in Brussels. He'd placed his 30,000 members at their disposal.

'I thought Staf de Clercq had been detained?'

'Yes,' Jef answered, 'and he was released a day later. You probably missed that news report.'

Pa Florent switched on the radio. Just then, the government announced to the Belgian people that King Leopold III – now a prisoner of war – would not be able to continue ruling; and so from now on, the Cabinet would exercise royal authority until a regent had been appointed. As long as the British and French continued to fight, the Belgian military would remain aligned with the Allies. Pa Florent, Jef and Pierre listened attentively to what was being said.

The occupying forces immediately began putting their military regime in place. One priority was integrating Belgium into the German war economy. The unemployed were enlisted to restore the infrastructure, and the Germans compelled a large number of Belgians to work in German factories. One day, Franske came home in tears. He'd witnessed a heart-rending drama in which a family had been torn apart. Pa Florent comforted his son.

Pa Florent had heard from his colleagues at the bank where he worked that many people had fled the country; that the port of Antwerp was immobilized and that the flow of raw materials had ground to a halt. That's why Belgian officials, bankers and industrialists had decided to meet to develop an emergency plan. The team agreed to a financial and economic policy, because the Belgian economy needed to keep functioning after the war. It wasn't possible to exclude the occupying forces completely, so they decided to produce a limited amount of materials for them. The production of weapons and ammunition, however, would be restricted to those manufactured for personal use. One of Pa Florent's co-workers said that the Germans had a stake in the Galopin Doctrine, as this economic policy became known, because both parties agreed to it.

Back on the Parklaan, Pa Florent and his friends discussed the Waffen-SS, who were recruiting Belgian military manpower, and the coverage in the newspapers, which was strongly influenced by the occupying forces. Gaston explained that the Belga news agency was being controlled and censored by a department within the German military command, and that from now on it would be known as 'Belgapress'.

The men had had enough of the Germans' cowardly techniques for lying to the people. They made up their minds to publish newspapers clandestinely in order to suppress German propaganda and to give the Belgians some courage and hope.

'May I help?' asked Pierre.

'You have to help, because you're one of us!' Gaston answered.

Pierre had agreed to meet up with his gang in the park. He said goodbye to his father's friends, ran up the stairs and fetched a revolver hidden in the secret double floor of his wardrobe. He cleaned the weapon with a woolen cloth while watching the German patrols from his window. Then he stuck the gun through his belt and pulled his sweater over it. He put on the hat he'd gotten from his father and rode his bike to the park. His friends were waiting for him at the entrance. The guys all liked his hat, and they all wanted one just like it.

'There's something else,' said Pierre, pulling up his sweater.

His friends were amazed, and they all claimed to have weapons stashed at home as well. Then Felix unbuttoned his shirt to show them the dagger he was hiding. Then they all started talking about the French, who had agreed to an armistice with Germany and Italy on 22 June. Two Germans came up to the group. The boys hadn't seen the soldiers approaching. Felix, who was a genius at math, happened to have an arithmetic book handy. He started working out a complicated formula aloud. The men in uniform pulled the book from his hands and thumbed through it. Their display of power didn't make much of an impression on Pierre, however. He looked the soldiers straight in the eyes and clenched his fists. Thanks to them, his father had been injured, and he'd lost his mother because of all the hardship.

'Don't do it,' whispered Felix, as he stood protectively in front of Pierre.

The schoolboys were given a severe talking to. After that the Germans broke up the meeting, because public gatherings had been prohibited.

Back home, some friends of Pa Florent were visiting. Pierre heard that a number of the Belgian ministers had chosen the side of Leopold III, while others had sought refuge in England. Pa Florent explained to his son that the command was now in the hands of Alexander von Falkenhausen, a general from the German infantry, and that the military administration had two military police forces at their disposal for maintaining order on Belgian soil. One was the 'Feldgendarmerie', who were uniformed military police, and the other was the 'Geheime Feldpolizei' or Secret Field Police.

'I refuse to submit to German authority. I hate the occupying forces!' shouted Pierre, who had just turned fifteen.

Eveline had heard Pierre's raised voice and urged him to calm down. Franske didn't understand much of what was going on and sat beside his father. Pierre went to his room, furious. That night, Pa Florent talked with his friends about Guernsey and Jersey, the British Channel Islands off the French coast, which had fallen into German hands.

Britain had turned down Germany's offer of peace. On 10 July, the Luftwaffe began bombing the British Isles; Churchill bombed Berlin in retaliation. The Germans then struck other large British cities. While Germany and Britain were being heavily attacked, war broke out in North Africa. Italian troops, using Libya as a base, invaded Egypt, which was under British control. Shortly thereafter the Italians assailed Greece, without having bothered to notify their allies. The invasion was a failure.

The Belgian national broadcasting system fell under the command of the German military administration. The Germans forbade the Belgians to listen to English radio broadcasts. A friend of Pa Florent's had it on good authority that it was becoming difficult to present unbiased reports. The Germans were bribing publishers and journalists, while the French and English were trying to get the press on their side by means of financial incentives.

It upset Pa Florent's group of visiting friends that the freedom of the press was being restricted. Gaston, who had connections within the Belga news agency, said: 'The agency hates transmitting German information, which is why the German embassy delivers sugar-coated news items directly to the papers.'

They talked throughout the night about how the Germans were contemptuously violating the freedom of the press, which had been guaranteed by the constitution. Some of them didn't make it home and spent the night at the Parklaan. Talk of the war began first thing the next morning. Celina had fetched a few newspapers, and the men compared the coverage in them. The papers reported that Minister Spaak had notified all the diplomats that the Belgian government, consisting of Albert de Vleeschauwer, Premier Hubert Pierlot, Paul Spaak and Camille Gutt, would be continuing operations from London. Pa Florent's friends stayed a while to discuss this. Then, before they left, Pa Florent invited his friends back for Christmas dinner.

Rubble was being cleared on a massive scale in Aalst. The Germans forced hundreds of unemployed people to assist the city's cleanup crew. The public squares, alleys and parks were all tidied up.

The friends celebrated Christmas together at the Parklaan. One of them had an art gallery which had been closed by the Germans. The man reported that the artist Albert Servaas sympathized with Hitler and had left for Germany, along with some others.

At New Year's it was always busy at the house on the Parklaan. Family and friends dropped in to wish Pa Florent a happy new year, because he couldn't get around very easily.

1941

It was quiet in Pierre's room, the only sound being the scratching of his pen. Throughout the year, he wrote down details of the war's events in the new notebook his father had given him for Christmas:

– In February 1941 Hitler had sent his top general, Erwin Rommel, to Libya with the German Africa Corps to back up the Italian allies and to drive the British out of North Africa.

– Two months later, the German and Italian armies advanced on Yugoslavia and Greece. Hitler wanted to restore order in the Balkans because of the defeat that Mussolini had suffered in Greece in 1940. An insurrection had broken out in the city of Belgrade because the Yugoslavian premier had signed the Tripartite Pact in Vienna on 25 March 1941; the uprising threatened to destabilize the entire region. Yugoslavia capitulated on 18 April 1941. The Greek Army surrendered a few days later. The German invasion forced the Allies to withdraw.

– While war was raging in the Balkans, Japan and Russia signed a neutrality pact – for five years – in April 1941 in Moscow.

– Operation Barbarossa began on 22 June 1941. The German Wehrmacht drove the Russians out of Poland and attacked the Soviet Union, in spite of the German-Soviet non-aggression pact of 1939. According to the press, it was the largest military advance in history. Italy and Romania also declared war on the Soviet Union. On 12 July 1941, an Anglo-Soviet Agreement had been signed in Moscow. The two countries pledged to assist each other in the fight against Germany. Stalin became the Commander in Chief of the Russian Army as of 5 August 1941.

Pierre looked up from his notebook and noticed that the rain had stopped. He put down his pen and went outside.

He ran into his friend de Rudder in town. The group of boys had stopped meeting in public after that incident with the German soldiers. De Rudder was much older than Pierre, and he encouraged him to join the BV Resistance group, made up of people from Aalst. Pierre was eager to know more. De Rudder explained it all to him in a café, and in that group Pierre behaved in a way that wasn't really appropriate for a boy of his youthful age – the lad was just fifteen. He would turn sixteen in July. His friend told him about Staf de Clercq, the leader of the VNV.

'My father says that de Clercq and his party are aligned with the collaboration.'

'Yes, that's true, but they couldn't persuade him to have his members take up arms to do Germany's bidding,' said de Rudder.

Pa Florent wouldn't allow his son to be seen with de Rudder, so from then on Pierre distanced himself from that group, which disbanded shortly thereafter.

Since his invasion of the Soviet Union, Hitler needed more military personnel. The Flemish National League, with German support, had absorbed the Flemish branch of the far-right Rexist Party and the remains of the ultra-Flemish Verdinaso Party in order to create the VNV. Their leader, de Clercq, then decided to go down the route of military collaboration, and established the Flemish Legion, which was made up of volunteers from the region of Flanders prepared to fight for the Germans. The SS had promised de Clercq that the Flemish troops would be trained by Dutch-speaking officers, would not become part of the Waffen-SS, and wouldn't be deployed at the front; de Clercq was allowed to choose the Legion's commander. Before long, the papers reported that the Flemish Legion wasn't receiving any special treatment at all. The SS's intentions soon became clear: they wanted to incorporate Flanders into the German Reich.

In the French-speaking regions of Belgium, there were also reports that a Walloon Legion had been set up by Léon Degrelle, the leader of the fascist Rexist Party. The Walloon leader personally took up arms. The newspapers said that the Walloon Legion had also been forced to comply with the will of the Germans. The Legion's troops were all given a German uniform and forced to pledge loyalty to Germany. The papers said that the Belgian legions were suffering enormous hardships. The military collaboration was a huge disappointment for de Clercq and Degrelle: it hadn't strengthened their position in the way they'd hoped.

Meanwhile, Pierre's friend de Rudder had transferred his allegiance to the National Socialist Motor Corps or NSKK, a paramilitary support organization that served as a supply unit for such groups as the Luftwaffe. When Pierre heard that de Rudder had gone over to the German camp, he felt disgusted. The urge to resist the occupying forces, combined with the hostile feelings towards fascism he had picked up at home, drove him to keep fighting for freedom and justice. He joined the Resistance and signed up with the group to which his friends Felix, Smekens, Eelbode and de Moor belonged. By then, they had all gotten hold of the same type of hat and long trench coat that Pierre had. They met regularly in the cellar of the Madelon banquet hall.

That winter, food, coal and wood all became scarce: everything was rationed, and on the black market the price of provisions shot through the roof. As a result, theft became rampant. Farmers set up patrols because their land was being plundered and their cattle were disappearing. Civilians were constantly on guard – things were being stolen everywhere. One night Eveline stormed into Pierre's room.

'Pierre, wake up!'

She shook him until he groggily opened his eyes.

Pierre sat straight up and hurried out of bed, because he heard something. He peeked through a gap in the heavy drapes. Eveline was petrified and her legs were trembling.

'Darn it,' Pierre said, 'there's a German climbing over the fence!'

When Eveline heard that she went to her room.

Pierre ran downstairs, grabbed a kitchen knife from the counter top and pulled open the back door with a jolt.

'Eveline?' asked the German soldier.

Pierre waved his weapon, and the man in uniform made a U-turn. Pierre heard his father coming and hid the knife. Pa Florent was just in time to see the man struggling over the fence and disappearing. He asked: 'What was that all about?'

'I don't know for sure. Maybe he wanted to steal something!' Pierre invented a story to spare his sick father's feelings, suffering as he did from the excruciating pain of incurable gangrene. Pierre was confronted with the Great War's terrible consequences on a daily basis.

Once his father had gone back to bed, Pierre stormed into his older sister's room. He gave her hell. Eveline swore blind that she didn't know the German.

Pierre had agreed to meet Gaston that morning. He was involved in the clandestine press and maintained close contact with Pa Florent. Because Pa Florent couldn't get around very easily, he had his son pick up the underground newspapers at Gaston's, either by bicycle or on foot. Gaston tied the papers around the boy's body so as not to attract attention. If Pierre ran into Germans on his way home, he usually made a detour. Sometimes there was no way around, and he had to pass by the occupying forces. Then he biked past as inconspicuously as possible, and whistled a tune to keep his nerves in check.

Back home, Pa Florent separated out the underground papers: *Free Belgium, Belgium Free,* and many others. Before long Pierre wasn't just the delivery boy, he was also distributing the papers to his friends and acquaintances. 'Read it and pass it on,' he said each time he handed someone a newspaper.

Soon afterwards, his whole gang became involved. At school the boys were able to communicate with each other freely. They bragged about how many German trucks they had sent to kingdom come. Pierre talked about weapons. He knew how he could get his hands on some pistols. He spent his savings on weapons to supply to his friends in the Resistance.

One day, Pierre was detained by two German soldiers, and was forced to stand against a wall and be searched. Luckily, he didn't have anything in his possession; he'd just handed over a weapon to somebody in the Resistance. Felix was on his way to Pierre's and saw the whole thing happen. He tried to turn back but then he found himself surrounded by Germans. He too was forced to stand against the wall and his pockets were emptied. But the Germans couldn't find anything on him either, so they let both boys go.

Later that night, Felix clambered over the fence at Pierre's house on the Parklaan. Pierre was waiting for him with a list of banned books which the Germans had removed from libraries and book-stores; the librarian had passed the list on to Pierre's father. The boys looked over the banned books, and noticed that they were all anti-German and Jewish works. He and Felix hurried to Pierre's room, where they hid the list in the secret double floor of his ward-robe.

Franske came home making a tremendous racket. Celina urged him to be quiet because Pa Florent was sleeping, but the boy wouldn't have any of it and woke his father. Franske told him that he'd once again seen people in town with a yellow star on the upper left-hand corner of their clothes. Pa Florent still looked dazed from his nap, but he sat bolt upright and said: 'That's the Star of David.'

'What an outrage! Every Jewish person older than six is required to wear the six-pointed star, to make them stand out from the rest of the population. Did you know that Jewish people aren't allowed out between eight o'clock in the evening and seven o'clock in the morning?' asked Pierre, as he let Felix out of the back door.

'I read that the Jews aren't permitted to move anywhere except Antwerp, Liege, Brussels or Charleroi,' his father added.

'What could possess the Germans to issue these kinds of rules?' Pierre wondered.

In the meantime, Franske had made a Star of David for himself. He stuck it on the upper left-hand side of his shirt and wanted to go out wearing it. Fortunately, Pierre was able to stop him. Pa Florent took away the star. Franske stormed up the stairs, furious.

One night, Pierre talked with his father about the failed landing at Dieppe, which had taken place in the summer of 1942. Pa Florent had heard that the British Prime Minister, Churchill, and the American President, Roosevelt, had been urged by Stalin to set up a second front on the European mainland, to keep the Germans away from the Eastern front. The Allies had hoped to use Operation Jubilee to break through the German coastal defense, a line stretching along the entire west coast of Europe. But the raid on Dieppe had failed: the invaders had been met with German mortar fire. Their tanks became bogged down on the beach, their vessels were blown to smithereens. Countless Canadian and British troops lost their lives or were taken prisoner. The RAF lost hundreds of planes.

'This war is far from over,' Pa Florent sighed. He turned up the radio because the announcer was saying that Staf de Clercq had died unexpectedly of a heart attack and had been replaced by Hendrik Elias. Following the obituary, it was announced that the Germans had reached the River Volga and that Stalingrad was being heavily bombed.

Pierre and his friends biked to the coast to see the notorious German Atlantic Wall for themselves. Hitler had reinforced that line of defense – which ran from Norway in the north to the south of France – by building thousands of bunkers, trenches and coastal batteries. The whole area was closely guarded, and the boys were stopped on their way there. They weren't allowed anywhere near the coast. They hadn't realized that stricter rules applied in the entire coastal area than inland. The Germans ordered them to turn back. Pierre brought his father and friends up to speed with the fact that they hadn't been permitted anywhere near the construction project. Celina had heard from her family that people who lived on the coast had been confined to a radius of just a few kilometers from where they lived, and that all access to dikes and beaches had been cut off.

'A pity we can't see such a gigantic project up close,' said Pierre, while looking at the front page of the paper dated 23 October 1942. 'Bernard Montgomery has become one of the new British commanders in Egypt.'

'Yes, I'd seen that in this morning's paper,' answered his father.

In November 1942 a broadcast announced that the people who'd assassinated Charleroi's Rexist Party mayor – a known German sympathizer – had not yet been found. In retribution, General von Falkenhausen granted permission for the execution of six hostages from near Charleroi, as well as two Communists from Antwerp, within the van Breendonk fort. They were all suspected of sabotage. In reaction, Pierre said: 'Executing hostages for unsolved acts of resistance goes against international law. It's forbidden by Article 50 of The Hague Convention of 1907.'

'That's something that's been happening in northern France. The occupying forces have already executed hostages in retaliation for unresolved acts of sabotage,' answered Pa Florent. He held up his hand to urge quiet, because an announcement was being made that the Belgian ministers in London strongly objected to the military occupation authority's introduction of obligatory employment in Belgium. The announcer went on to say that American and British troops had invaded the French colonies of Morocco and Algeria.

Pa Florent nodded off to sleep after all these significant reports, thanks to the strong medication he had taken for the pain. Celina turned off the radio. The house became quiet and Pierre went up to his room with one of his friends, who had arrived through the back door. As they went up the stairs, the teenagers talked about the Board of Directors at the University of Brussels, who had canceled all lectures because of the appointment of a World War One collaborator. The boys glanced out of the window, where the Germans were patrolling in the street.

It was cold, but sunny. Franske and Emilienne dropped in at Uncle Jef's place. To their enormous surprise, they walked in on Jef's wife sitting on the lap of a German commander. They were singing German songs and drinking champagne. The children raced home. Once they got back, Emilienne shook her father awake. Franske and Emilienne both started talking at once.

'Slow down, kids, I can't understand what you're saying. You first, Emilienne.'

'Aunt Maria was just sitting on a German's lap!'

'They were singing German songs and drinking champagne,' Franske promptly added.

'Sacre bleu!' exclaimed Pa Florent.

Franske hurried to Pierre to tell him what he'd seen.

'Franske, go be funny somewhere else!' ordered Pierre.

Pierre looked up from his book as Emilienne appeared in the doorway and said: 'It's true!' Pierre went as white as a sheet, threw his book on the floor, ran downstairs and grabbed his sweater from the coat rack. He slammed the door behind him. When he turned into the Zoutstraat, he saw a German officer leaving Uncle Jef's fur shop. Pierre went in.

'Where's Uncle Jef?'

'He's gone to see your father,' Aunt Maria answered.

The boy turned right around. You could hear Jeff and Florent arguing from the street. In the hallway, Pierre ran into his uncle and calmly said: 'I never want to see you again, Uncle Jef.'

'Now listen, Pierre!' Pierre slammed the door in his face.

The argument hit them all like a ton of bricks.

Gustaaf's asthma had been brought under control, so he was given permission to go home to celebrate Christmas with his brothers and sisters. Pa Florent had given Celina money to buy the ingredients for their Christmas dinner on the black market. During the holidays, she always got a little extra cash to buy something for herself.

German soldiers were swarming around the house. This made Pa Florent uneasy. He sensed that something was up. Earlier that day, a German soldier had been chatting with Franske. The soldier gave him a few coins to go and buy him some Dutch doughnuts at the stand around the corner. Franske figured out that the German soldier wanted to get him out of the way, away from the front of the house where he lived. So instead of buying the doughnuts, he doubled back and climbed over the fence surrounding their back garden. He showed the money to his father. At that, Pa Florent ordered Franske to go throw his dagger into the River Dender, and he sent Emilienne along with him.

'Be careful!' Pa Florent whispered.

A little later, the kids disappeared over the concrete fence surrounding the garden. Franske had the dagger under his pullover. They had to cross the street to get to the Dender, but two soldiers were blocking the way. Franske wanted to turn back, but Emilienne grabbed her little brother's hand and kept going, strolling as inconspicuously as possible. The boy didn't dare look at the men in uniform.

'That dagger's got to go!' Emilienne said in a hushed voice.

The kids arrived at the Dender Bridge and they made a little detour. When they got to the riverbank, Franske took out the dagger, which his father had wrapped in newspaper. He threw the weapon into the water and it sank straight to the bottom.

Pa Florent was waiting for the children to return, and Gustaaf had clambered onto a barrel so he could see over the fence.

'Here they come!' Gustaaf bellowed.

Pa Florent breathed a sigh of relief when he saw them.

'Mission accomplished,' said Franske proudly.

That night, Celina served their Christmas dinner. The argument with Uncle Jef clouded the occasion. There was a little something for everyone beneath the Christmas tree.

The days that followed were uneventful. Emilienne read the book she'd been given, Eveline was over the moon about the nylon stockings she'd found as her Christmas present, and Franske and Gustaaf were busy divvying up pieces of candy. Pa Florent gazed upon his brood, satisfied, and yet there was something he couldn't quite put his finger on, something bothering him. Pierre had just returned home. He'd been delivering ammunition for two revolvers and a pistol he'd supplied to Scheerlinck, who was in the Armée Secrète. He went to his room, because his father was expecting a visitor.

A little while later, Pa Florent was visited by an Englishman who was connected with the British Prime Minister. The Englishman and Pa Florent had known each other since childhood because their fathers had been good friends. The Englishman passed on confidential information; he, along with a few other English pilots, was hiding in the cellars of the Terlinden Castle, which belonged to a friend of Pa Florent.

Just then, Celina returned from town. She opened the door and Franske, who had been running after her the whole day, sprung inside ahead of her. She said hello to the visitor and started complaining about the price of butter, which had shot through the roof. Pa Florent got annoyed and sent Celina and Franske to the kitchen. The Englishman didn't want to take up any more of his friend's time, but before he left he took an envelope addressed to Pierre from his inside pocket and handed it to Pa Florent. The letter had traveled with someone's family to Ireland, was then smuggled into England, and was given to Pa Florent's friend by another Brit.

Pierre was in the kitchen getting a glass of water when Pa Florent handed him the envelope. It was from Johanna, his American pen pal. Elated, Pierre went up to his room. He sat on the bed, opened the letter and read:

Hello Pierre,
The sun is shining here and the temperature has climbed above 86° F. I'm writing this letter on the terrace. I've been saving clippings for you about the war from the American newspapers, and will include them with my letter. Here's a summary of the events:

– On 7 December 1941 the newspapers wrote that the Japanese had delivered a heavy blow to the United States. Many Americans died during the surprise attack on Pearl Harbor. Much of the American fleet had been sunk, and many airplanes were shot down. Japanese troops had landed on Malacca, Burma and Malaysia at the same time. The Americans declared war on Japan. Hitler declared war on

the United States a few days later. After the surprise attack on Pearl Harbor, the Americans and British watched as the Japanese, who already occupied Korea and a large part of China, continued their attack on European and American territories in the Far East.

Pierre stopped reading, put down the letter, and went downstairs. He sat beside his father and asked: 'Where is Pearl Harbor?'

'Pearl Harbor is an American naval base in the Hawaiian port of Oahu, in the Pacific Ocean.'

'But why has Hitler declared war on the United States? Wasn't it the Japanese who attacked Pearl Harbor?!'

'Yes, but Germany, Italy and Japan had signed the Tripartite Pact in Berlin on 27 September 1940. Some of the Balkan states also aligned themselves with the Axis powers by signing the treaty. In the Tripartite Pact, Germany promised to support Japan in its conflicts with other countries. Moreover, Germany was already furious with the United States, because on 11 March 1941 President Roosevelt had signed the Lend-Lease Bill, which made it possible to offer material support to the United Kingdom and other countries actively working to stop Hitler and his followers.'

'Why did the Japanese attack an American naval base?'

Pa Florent went to look for the English-language newspapers his British friend had carefully saved for him. While searching through the papers for reports of preceding hostilities, he explained that the Japanese needed reserves of raw materials, and that tension between the United States and Japan had been growing even before the attack on Pearl Harbor. Japan had been conducting an aggressive policy of expansion for some years; reports of the relentless cruelty of which the Japanese Army was guilty circulated around the globe. The Americans were keeping a close eye on the Japanese, but Roosevelt's hands were tied by his country's policy of neutrality and he could only impose economic sanctions on Japan. In January

1940, he had had the entire Pacific Fleet moved from California to Hawaii in order to exert pressure on Japan.'

Pa Florent pulled the newspapers out of the pile and handed them to his son. Pierre took the English reading matter to his room, and placed it beside his bed. He sat down and continued reading the letter from America:

– *In December 1941, the papers here reported that the Netherlands had declared war on Japan on 8 December. The Japanese had invaded Java along its north coast.*

– *In January 1942, there were reports that the Japanese had landed on the British Solomon Islands. They drove out the British and occupied the township of Rabaul, a port city of strategic importance. The occupying forces were planning to isolate the Allied troops in the United States, Australia and New Zealand.*

– *On 17 February 1942, the American papers reported that the British had suffered a crushing defeat. The Japanese had succeeded in seizing the city of Singapore. That city has an important deep-water port accessible to heavy warships. American, British, Dutch and Australian commandos all used it.*

– *It says here that in March 1942 the Allied troops surrendered on Java. As a result, important sources of oil and rubber fell into Japanese hands. The Allies were unable to prevent the fall of the Dutch East Indies.*

– *In April 1942, it was reported that the Americans had succeeded in surreptitiously entering Japanese waters with their aircraft carriers* Enterprise *and* Hornet. *The surprise attack on Pearl Harbor was still fresh in their minds, and the Doolittle Raid was launched.*

Bombers took off from the American aircraft carrier to carry out a reprisal attack on Tokyo. It was the first American air attack on the Japanese mainland. I later learned that the attack had been named after Lieutenant Colonel James Doolittle, who planned and led the attack.

– *At the end of April 1942, the papers published word that the Japanese fleet had been sighted in the West Pacific. They were intending to attack the Solomon Islands and New Guinea. The Americans had intercepted this information and sent the aircraft carriers USS* Lexington *and USS* Yorktown *to the Sea of Japan.*

– *The daily papers reported: on 6 May 1942 the Island of Corregidor, the last American stronghold in the Philippines, capitulated.*

– *In May, reports said that both the Japanese and the Americans had suffered heavy losses during the Battle of the Coral Sea. The Americans lost a fleet oil tanker, a destroyer and the USS* Lexington *aircraft carrier. The USS* Yorktown *aircraft carrier was critically damaged but remained operational. Two of the Japanese aircraft carriers were heavily damaged. Yet the Americans had nothing to complain about. They'd prevented a southern invasion of New Guinea and kept the Solomon Islands from falling completely into the hands of the enemy.*

– *You must read this article! Here is a summary: the brilliant American military intelligence service had discovered that the Japanese were planning an attack on the Midway Atoll, which housed an American naval base. The Americans used Midway as a stopover for operations in the Pacific. The position of the ring-shaped island, in the middle of the Pacific and halfway between North America and Asia, was a location the Japanese coveted. The Japanese Navy*

appeared in the Pacific with their fleet, which included four aircraft
carriers, but the Americans were prepared for the attack. Three air-
craft carriers were lying in wait to the north of the islands – the
Enterprise, *the* Hornet *and the* Yorktown *– along with the rest of*
the fleet, ready to strike at the order of Admiral Chester W. Nimitz,
Commander of the Pacific Fleet. Fighting broke out on 4 June 1942.
American dive bombers hit three of the four Japanese aircraft carri-
ers, turning them into floating infernos. Japanese dive bombers were
still able to take off from the heavily damaged Japanese carrier, the
Hiryu. *Two American aircraft carriers were hit. A Japanese sub-*
marine brought down the aircraft carrier Yorktown. *It sunk on the*
morning of 7 July 1942. A destroyer, more than 100 airplanes and
a carrier were lost, and more than 200 American troops perished
during this naval battle. Their eternal rest awaited them at the bot-
tom of the ocean. In the end, the Japanese lost thousands of military
forces, all their aircraft carriers, hundreds of planes and one heavy
cruiser, while another was severely damaged. The Japanese planes
had failed to put the American base out of commission. The Japa-
nese did not take Midway. The US Pacific Fleet remained intact.
With that, Japan's offensive position came to a definite end.

– *In August 1942 the papers reported that the Allies had launched a*
counter-attack in New Guinea. The Americans landed on Guadal-
canal and a few neighboring islands.

– *It's now September 1942, and the battle continues undiminished on*
land, at sea and in the air.

These are just the main facts concerning what's happened so far. After
Japan's failed attack on Midway, there were hardly any more reports
in the papers. I look forward to your next letter and I'll try to keep you
up to date. I'll be spending my upcoming vacation with my family in

*Ireland. I hope you can come and see me then. Hope to hear from you
soon!*

Warmest best wishes,
Johanna
Virginia, September 1942

Pierre stuck the letter, which had taken almost three months to
reach him, into his notebook and hid it under his mattress so no
one would find it. Before he left his room, he glanced through the
window at the Germans patrolling the street. Pierre was cold. He
went downstairs and sat by the fire. Pa Florent stirred the coals and
asked Celina to bring the boy something warm. He then wrapped a
blanket that had been lying on the arm of the couch around Pierre's
shoulders, and sat beside him. Pierre started talking about the anti-
fascist student group in which he was active. Then he turned up the
radio to listen to an important announcement. The international
news was completely devoted to the war. The English station reported that the Germans were suffering losses on all fronts. The
announcer said that General Rommel's triumph in recapturing the
port city of Tobruk from the British had been short-lived, because
Field Marshal Montgomery had defeated Rommel at El Alamein.
Rommel had been forced to beat a hasty retreat with his German
and Italian troops. Next, the announcer described the battle raging around the Solomon Islands, where the Allies were making sure
Japan wouldn't be able to cut off Australia and New Zealand from
the United States. In closing, there were reports about the heavy
fighting raging on the Eastern front. The Russians had begun a big
winter offensive and the Germans were suffering losses. The Soviets
were doing everything in their power to drive back the Germans
and their Axis supporters. When the news was over, Pierre turned
off the radio. He told his father what he'd read in the letter from
America.

THE ARREST

The arrival of Pierre's friend Felix, who came in through the back, cut their discussion short.

'I didn't dare ring the bell. The place is swarming with German soldiers! I crawled over your back fence.'

'It's been like that for a few days,' Pierre answered as he peeked through the curtains.

Felix said in a hushed voice that Smekens, one of their gang, had been picked up by the German military police.

'When?'

'This morning. He was still in bed!'

'What's going on?' asked Pa Florent.

'Smekens was dragged out of bed this morning by the Feldgendarmerie,' he whispered quietly to his father.

'Sacre bleu!' exclaimed Pa Florent.

'We need to go to the Madelon to warn the others,' said Pierre, pulling on his coat.

'Why the Madelon?' Pa Florent wanted to know.

'We agreed to meet there, in the basement, if there was ever any trouble,' answered Pierre.

The boys didn't dare leave through the front door because the Germans were keeping a close eye on it, so they clambered over the garden fence out at the back. When they got closer to town they noticed that German soldiers were following them, so they slipped into an alley to shake them off.

They holed up in the doorway of an old house belonging to someone they knew. There Felix lifted the grate leading to the cellar, and they were able to slip through the opening and scramble down to the ancient labyrinth of underground passageways which shot off in all directions, forming a link between the street's various monasteries. Felix shined his flashlight through the damp, dark and chilly passageways. The boys trudged through the water in the tunnel leading to the central market square. There was a grille at the end. Pierre looked through the fretwork and saw the black boots of a German soldier pacing back and forth.

'We have to turn back; the Jerries are everywhere!'

Pierre and Felix went back to the narrow lane, but by then the Germans had gone, so they took a circuitous route to the central market square. They saw that a German was guarding the entrance to the Madelon.

'There's an iron hatch at the back for lowering barrels of beer into the cellar. Maybe we can get in that way,' suggested Felix.

They circled around. From a distance, they could see that German soldiers were standing watch there, as well. They had to turn back yet again. Members of the Feldgendarmerie came around the corner, leading away one of their friends: the desperate look in the boy's eyes spoke volumes. Felix wiped away a tear, and Pierre choked back his feelings. Now they were certain someone had betrayed them.

Back home, Pa Florent noticed that Pierre was unusually quiet and asked: 'Something wrong?'

'The Feldgendarmerie have nabbed another of my friends.'

'Sacre bleu!' Pa Florent swore, and he urged his son to go into hiding for a while with relatives in Brussels.

Pierre refused to run from the occupying forces. He didn't want to leave his father behind. Someone pounded on the door just as Pa Florent was about to throw the clandestine newspapers into the fire. Pierre didn't even have time to open up. The German secret police had climbed over the concrete fence and stormed in through the back. They thrust a pistol against Florent's head and wrenched the underground papers out of his hands.

'Run, Pierre! Run!' he bellowed.

Pierre made a grab for the German holding his father at gunpoint. One of the soldiers hit him with his rifle butt, and Pierre fell to the floor. Emilienne and Franske ran crying up the stairs and hid under the bed. Celina and Eveline were already hiding in the cellar. The Germans emptied the drawers and cupboards. They cut open the lining of the couch and easy chairs. They asked Pierre where he'd hidden the weapons. When he didn't answer, they hit him, hard.

'Somebody spilled the beans,' thought Pierre.

The German repeated his question in a more authoritarian tone, but it still had no result: Pierre remained silent. Franske and Emilienne heard the soldiers coming up the stairs. They lay motionless until they were dragged out from under the bed. Emilienne lost control. One of the Germans held the little girl in check, at which Franske stood in front of him, fists clenched, shouting: 'Let my sister go!'

The German smiled; then he boxed Franske's ear and ordered him to get on his knees and face the wall. They searched the entire house until they finally found three of the six revolvers with ammunition hidden between the rafters under the roof. Pierre was apprehended for hiding weapons, expressing hostility views towards the Germans, and possessing clandestine newspapers. An SS officer threw the notebook he'd found in Pierre's room – containing all his writings – into the fire; Pierre watched it being devoured by flames. One of the German officers said that they'd shoot Pa Florent some other time, because for now he was too difficult to move. At that, Pierre spat at the officer. Pa Florent cried as they led his son away. Pierre had never seen his father cry before.

'I'll be back, Papa!' he shouted.

While the military police led the lad through the streets with his hands over his head, bystanders watched, outraged. They pelted the German military police with stones, and the man who held Pierre at gunpoint was hit on the head with a rock. The culprits were rounded up by the secret police and hauled away. Pierre was taken to German Headquarters in Aalst.

THE NIEUWE WANDELING PRISON IN GHENT

Pierre was transferred, after a brief interrogation, to the Nieuwe Wandeling prison in Ghent. The military government had incorporated the prison into the German system of repression and had requisitioned the lowest tiers of the A and B wings to lock up their prisoners.

When Pierre arrived at the penal institution he was pushed into a registration office where his name was written in the logbook. He was forced to hand over the clothes he was wearing and all of his other personal effects. He was given a number and a prisoner's uniform. A medical examination followed. His head was shaved for hygienic reasons. Before he was brought to his cell, he met with the German in charge of this cell block, an area that was forbidden terrain for the Belgian staff of the prison. The tier had been closed off from the Belgian cell blocks by a wooden partition with a bolted door. A German was standing guard. From that moment on, Pierre understood that the enemy had robbed him of his freedom. He read the prison rules hanging on the whitewashed wall of his cell as the heavy door slammed shut behind him. There were regulations for everything: it all had to be done in a certain way. The teenager clambered onto his folding iron bed, which had been opened up to become a table, and looked through the small window set high in the inside wall. From there he could just make out a part of the inner courtyard. He'd read in the prison regulations that it was forbidden to look out of the window. You'd get a heavy penalty if you were caught, but he wasn't worried about that. He

clambered down from the bed and sat on the wooden chair, survey-
ing the washbasin, the chamber pot and the locker. Then he folded
open the bed, lay down and crossed his arms behind his head. He
stared at the ceiling and said to himself: 'Smekens was the first one
arrested. Maybe they forced him to betray us.'

As the evening's darkness gradually descended on his cold,
cramped prison cell, Pierre listened to the strange and unpleas-
ant sounds coming from the corridor. It seemed as if a mysteri-
ous whirlwind was racing manically through his head. He closed
his eyes and dreamed of his father walking through the park with
his mother, brothers and sisters. Franske was beckoning him, but
Pierre jolted awake just as he was about to join his family. He looked
around, terrified, and slowly realized he'd been locked up.

Aalst
There was a huge sense of outrage at the house on the Parklaan. Pa
Florent was inconsolable – yet another heavy blow to bear. Franske
and Emilienne secretly made their way to Uncle Jef's. Franske led
the way into the shop, bellowing: 'The Jerries have taken Pierre!'

Jef was shocked. He pulled on his jacket and rushed to his brother's. Pa Florent was furious when he saw Jef standing in the doorway; Celina had just poured him a glass of whiskey and he threw it
at Jef's head. Pa Florent accused Jef of being a hypocrite, while Jef
tried to calm Pa Florent down.

'Calm down, you say! The Krauts have got their hands on my son,
while you're trying to do their bidding. Just to be opportunistic!'

'There's a war on, Florent, and it doesn't look like we'll win!' That
was hard for Pa Florent to stomach. 'Florent, I'm trying to save the
business. You know I'm upset about what's happened to Pierre. I'll
do everything I can to save him.'

'Jef, get out of here. I want you out of my house, right now!'

Jef left the house on the Parklaan. He couldn't hold back his tears and walked through the streets, sobbing. Once he got home, he went straight to bed.

The Nieuwe Wandeling prison

Around six in the morning, a bell rang through the corridors of the prison. Pierre jolted awake, jumped up, made his bed according to the prescribed regulations and freshened up with what little water was available. The chamber pots were collected at the same time as the breakfast was handed out. No words were exchanged. Breakfast consisted of a piece of bread and something to drink. Pierre hid the bread in his folding bed because he couldn't manage to choke down a single mouthful. He took one sip of the filthy beverage and had to spit it out immediately.

Later in the morning, Pierre heard the sound of locks being unbolted. He could hear the prisoners and guards in the corridor. He climbed up on the folding bed to look through his little window.

'The prisoners are being let out in the yard,' he said to himself.

Pierre climbed down off the bed. He bit his fingernail into a sharp point and carved the date of his arrest into the whitewashed wall.

It was cold: the radiator pipes running through his cell felt warm to the touch, but that wasn't enough to heat the place properly. To get some exercise he did a handstand, then a headstand, and then a handstand again. From that angle, he could see snowflakes whirling past the small window. Pierre stood up and climbed onto his folding bed to see the snowflakes more closely.

'How amazing – truly a miracle,' he whispered.

The noise in the corridor told him that the prisoners were back from their time in the yard. Towards midday, the inmates were each given a watery bowl of soup. Pierre found the prison food disgusting, but because he hadn't eaten for a while he took the bread he'd hidden that morning, soaked it in the soup and forced it down.

The hours in his cell passed as slowly as molasses. To kill time, he thought about all the books he'd read back home. While he was lost in thought the lights went on, and the evening meal was shoved through the door. It consisted of a scoop of cooked potatoes and some vegetables. Sometime around ten, the lights went out.

On his sixth day in prison, Pierre was picked up by the German secret police for questioning. He was brutally interrogated at their headquarters – punched, kicked, humiliated, locked up in a cramped pen and interrogated again. After the questioning, he was sent back to the Nieuwe Wandeling prison. There, Pierre was forced to walk laps around the yard deep into the night. Felix peeked through the window of his cell and saw how badly his friend had been beaten. Pierre kept staggering around the inner courtyard until he collapsed.

The next morning, Pierre woke up on the floor of his cell. He grabbed hold of the chair to pull himself up. His head was pounding, and he had aches and pains all over his body. He could hardly breathe because of the congealed blood in his nose. He used some water to wash the evidence of the interrogation from his face. Another prisoner was on duty handing out that morning's breakfast. Pierre was so thirsty he gulped down the hideous brew that accompanied the bread. When he put down his food bag, he noticed a piece of crumpled paper in it. He unfolded it and read: 'Take care! Felix!'

The pain made him stifle his smile.

'I've got to get rid of that note immediately,' he said to himself.

He stuck the crumpled paper in his mouth and tried to swallow it, but he couldn't choke it down. He spit it out, tore it into small pieces and managed to force it down with some breadcrumbs.

Pierre was locked up alone in his solitary cell for days on end. One morning, the door to his cell was unbolted.

'Ausgang,' shouted one of the guards from the corridor.

The inmates were allowed outside for a brief time. Because the investigation into Pierre's activities was still underway, he was confined to a small, cramped, open space between two buildings, surrounded by bars. From there he could see the other inmates walking silently around the yard, staying a safe distance from each other. He was hoping to catch a glimpse of Felix, but his friend was nowhere to be seen. Pierre was startled by one prisoner's screams. Two guards were giving him a beating because he'd picked something up off the ground. Pierre turned his back on the violence and looked up at the clear, blue sky. He remembered what he'd read about the goddess Athena, who, within the world of the gods, had power over everything that happened in the heavens. Pierre got lost in his daydreams, but the sharp north wind snapped him back to reality. He was cold in his prisoner's togs. It was below freezing and the yard time was lasting longer than it usually did. Finally, the inmates were locked in their cells again. Pierre shivered. He was chilled to the bone, and he did some exercises to warm up. That afternoon, lunch consisted of soup; the watery brew had a disgusting taste, but he drank every drop of it all the same.

A few weeks later, Pierre was again taken for questioning, and again he was severely beaten because he wouldn't answer the questions they asked him. The boy collapsed from the Germans' brutality.

Two days later, a guard nudged him with his foot. The man then threw water in Pierre's face because he hadn't gotten any response. Pierre regained consciousness. He felt completely spent. It was ice-cold and dark in his cell; his entire body was shaking. Pierre tried to concentrate on his breathing to stop his mind from whirling, but it was no use. Thoughts of his friend Felix, who'd had the courage to send him a note, kept running through his head, and that gave him the strength to stand up again. The lights were turned on in his cell. That evening Pierre was given some potatoes and a little chard. He managed to eat every bite. After that, he lay down on his bed and stared at the crucifix on the whitewashed wall. 'If the God we worship were a real God, he would never have created that psychopath Hitler, and he wouldn't allow all these atrocities be committed,' he thought to himself.

The next morning the Nieuwe Wandeling prison was in uproar, because someone had tacked a pamphlet to the door of the German warden's office. It was one of the thousands of pamphlets that had been dropped over Belgium months earlier, meant to give the population some moral support. No one knew who had smuggled in the pamphlet, and who had hung it up in the German block of the prison. It contained articles about Great Britain, and about the American help that had been promised to the Belgian people; there were pictures of Belgian soldiers as well. The German prison warden in charge of that cell block strode through the corridors screaming and cursing because one of his superiors was on his way to pay a visit. They combed through all the cells as quickly as they could but found nothing.

Sometime before noon, the Gestapo marched through the prison's corridors. Pierre heard them coming in his direction. The door of his cell swung open, and he was taken away for questioning. On his way to the interrogation center in Ghent he thought carefully about what he'd said during the previous cross-examinations, and what he'd kept to himself. The injuries he'd received during his previous bout of questioning were still clearly visible. Pierre was forced to wait on a chair in the corridor. He could hear the German agents ranting and raving, and their victims groaning and screaming. The interrogation they were conducting seemed to go on forever. Pierre spent hours on that wooden chair in the hallway, listening to what was happening inside.

When the doors of the interrogation room finally swung open, Pierre couldn't believe his eyes. His friends Scheerlinck and de Moor were sitting on a bench. Both men looked like they'd taken a beating, and were staring straight ahead. Pierre was told to sit down beside them on the bench, to their left. Two men from the SS were standing on either side. One of them made a fist and repeatedly punched the palm of his black-gloved hand. The man in front asked the boy how he knew Scheerlinck and de Moor. Pierre explained their relationship and told them about some of the things they'd done together. The man behind the table frowned and looked straight at Pierre. He lit a cigar, blew the smoke out in rings, and asked: 'Aren't you forgetting something?'

Pierre shook his head. Then the German hollered: 'You provided Scheerlinck with two revolvers and a gun with ammunition, and followed that with the criminal acts involving de Moor.'

The boys were confronted with each other. Pierre saw right away that Scheerlinck hadn't told them everything. He admitted that he'd given his friends weapons and ammunition.

'But I didn't sell them weapons and ammunition. I gave them away,' Pierre stressed.

He kept the rest of their secrets to himself. Pierre hadn't told the truth right away, so his friends were forced to beat him up. He was ordered to appear before a German court martial.

When Pierre was brought back to his cell in the Nieuwe Wandeling, he passed an inmate in the corridor who was being led away by the German military police. He glanced in the prisoner's direction and recognized Felix's father, who was a good friend of his own father. Back in his cell, Pierre made a mental list of the names of those he was sure had been detained: 'Felix, Smekens, de Moor, Scheerlinck and Felix's father.'

It was cold and dark in his cell. He'd missed his meals because of the interrogation. He took out a crust of bread and nibbled it in bed. He thought about his friends, who had been coerced into betraying him. But there were still things none of them had let out of the bag. The experience kept him awake the entire night.

Aalst

The house on the Parklaan was still a hotbed of resistance. Pa Florent made no bones about his hatred of the occupying forces. Resistance fighters visited the house regularly to pass on the information they'd obtained. That particular day, they were busy editing texts for the clandestine newspapers, and collecting money for printing. The meetings still ended the usual way. The men smoked cigars while Pa Florent played some music on his cello. One of the fellows reported as he was leaving that Stalin had just appointed Georgy Zhukov, a man who would stop at nothing, as Chief of General Staff of the Soviet Army.

Things with Eveline were going from bad to worse. Emilienne had the feeling her sister was up to no good. She moved her father's supply of morphine to prevent her sister from stealing it. Eveline went to tell her father she'd found a job in Brussels, one that included a place for her to live.

'That's fine, but if it doesn't work out, you come straight home. Understood?' Pa Florent said unsuspectingly, as he slipped his daughter some money.

The sick man went sadly to his room. As Eveline was about to go out of the door, Emilienne caught her trying to steal the morphine again.

'Eveline, don't you have any shame?'

'It's for a good cause!' Eveline whispered, and disappeared.

The young woman moved to the village of St Gilles, on the outskirts of Brussels. She registered with the municipality, as was required in Belgium at that time, and sent confirmation of this to her father. She gave the morphine she'd stolen to her friend, who brought the medication to a German field hospital that had run out. A few days later, Eveline left for Germany with an officer whose father was a judge, but she remained registered as a resident of St Gilles.

Celina was glad Eveline had left because she was a regular source of trouble in the family, but Pa Florent was having a hard time. He brought his son Gustaaf home again to make up for missing his daughter. The boy's asthma had been brought under control.

The car bringing Gustaaf home stopped in front of the house. Franske went outside to help his brother with the luggage. He was allowed to carry the suitcase, but Gustaaf preferred to carry his book bag himself. Pa Florent's face lit up when he saw the boy arrive, and he looked happier than anyone had seen him in ages. Gustaaf went to sit beside his father at the table right away and took some folders out of his brown leather book bag. His coin collection was in one folder, his valuable stamp collection in the other. Pa Florent had yet again managed to get his hands on a few old coins and postage stamps. He added them to the collection. Franske and Emilienne weren't allowed to touch these small objects. They examined them through a magnifying glass. Pa Florent stared at the stamp printed with a portrait of Leopold III.

'This blasted war!' he said to himself.

The last words Pierre had said during his arrest remained engraved in his memory. They echoed through his head, especially when things were quiet. That's when he often heard Pierre saying: 'I'll be back, Papa!'

For Pa Florent, his son's capture by the SS was almost too much to bear. He was a sick man, and he had to cope with a lot. There was an article in the papers saying that the bloodthirsty Hitler was pressuring German judges to impose crueler sentences – that hadn't escaped his attention. His brother Jef was also miserable because of his nephew's arrest; he was trying to bribe the German judges to save Pierre from the death penalty by giving them the most expensive fur coats from his shop. It was a delicate tightrope act because the insane German leader had threatened to suspend any judges who handed out lenient sentences.

THE CONVICTION

A few weeks later, Pierre was transferred from the Nieuwe Wandeling prison to the law courts in Ghent for his court martial. The boy appeared alone before the court, unlike the other detainees. Pierre was found guilty of possessing weapons and was sentenced to twenty-five months' imprisonment.

Aalst

Jef was notified immediately of the verdict and rushed to his brother's house. The family were relieved to hear that Pierre hadn't been sentenced to death. Pa Florent was aware of how difficult things would become for his son and said: 'I want to see him!'

'Pierre has been completely shut off from the outside world. He's not permitted to receive any visitors,' replied Jef.

'I want to see my son!' Pa Florent repeated.

He took his formal request from the desk drawer and handed it to Jef.

'I'll make some inquiries and see if there's any chance of visiting him,' Uncle Jef promised.

Celina had just gotten back from town, and from under her cape she produced groceries she'd managed to buy on the black market. She said that while she was out she'd heard that the Allies had landed on Sicily.

Everyone hoped that these difficult times would quickly come to an end. Jef and Pa Florent talked about the Resistance's spectacular attack on Paul Colin, the editor-in-chief of some publications sympathetic to Germany.

'Did you know, Florent, that they hanged the nineteen-year-old who'd been responsible, along with his two buddies?'

Suddenly, a heavily loaded truck rumbled through the street. The hellish racket scared the family half to death. They looked out of the window and saw a truck – laden with church bells – that had gotten stuck.

'Those are the bells from the Church of St Joseph! They're still negotiating to save the bells of the Church of St Martin. I hope they succeed because those bells are genuine art treasures,' Jef explained.

The German weapons industry was contending with a shortage of raw materials, so all the bells had been removed from the church towers within the German Reich. They were then melted down to provide the factories with iron. That wasn't enough, however, to keep the weapons industry going, so the Germans also confiscated bells from occupied areas. The people who lived nearby tried to prevent that from happening; they hid the keys to the churches, barricaded the entrances to the towers and threw stones at the workers who came to remove the bells. Church leaders, who tried to avoid ruffling the Nazis' feathers, nevertheless protested about the removal of the bells. The Bishop of Liège refused to hand over the keys to the Cathedral, but the Germans showed no mercy. They battered down the heavy doors and carted the bells away.

The Nieuwe Wandeling prison

After months of solitary confinement, Pierre was getting used to the monotonous prison routine. As his father often said: 'You can get used to anything!' Now he was starting to see the truth in that saying.

It was never quiet in his cell. Pierre attempted to develop a system of communication with the other inmates through the heat-ing pipes, and used the pipes to listen in on conversations between other prisoners; he managed to hear that the German troops had surrendered in Stalingrad and that German and Italian military forces had ceased fighting in Tunisia.

Pierre often counted the tally marks he had carved on the wall. That day he muttered '23 August 1943!' to himself.

He hopped off his folding bed because the conversation he heard in the corridor was heading in his direction. The cell door was un-bolted, and Pierre was led to a small room at the entrance to the prison. There, his things were thrown at him. Pierre got dressed and tightened his belt. His trousers hung loosely around his waist. He was led towards the train, along with a few others facing a simi-lar fate. Once the railcar was packed full with prisoners, its doors were shoved closed. It was a long time before the train started to move. When they arrived at St Gilles station near Brussels, SS of ficers were waiting for the convicts on the platform. They were led into St Gilles prison, accompanied by the sound of shouting. Pierre was locked up in a cell. He was allowed to keep his civilian clothes on. German civil servants were carrying files back and forth the whole day. The clerks were busy filling in forms. The following morning, the boy was taken from his cell and brought to the prison warden's office, where he was surprised by an unexpected visit from his family. The emotions at that encounter ran high. Pierre was sur-rounded by German soldiers and had to keep a certain distance from his family. Franske wanted to give his brother a package of cookies, but the Germans wouldn't allow it. Pa Florent exchanged a few quick words with his son. The visit was very brief. Afterwards, Pierre was led away. The whole experience left a deep impression on Pa Florent.

MERKPLAS, BELGIUM

An hour later, Pierre and the other prisoners were again brought to St Gilles station. The boy listened to the other prisoners' wide range of experiences. It soon became clear to him that some had been arrested because they were driven by idealism, whereas others had been motivated by a quest for adventure. They were all shoved into a railcar. When it was full to bursting, the doors were slid shut. The inmates had no idea of their destination. Rays of sunlight crept in through the slats. There was a thick layer of stinking hay on the floor. The prisoners were packed together like sardines. It was unbearably hot in there, and Pierre thought he would suffocate, but when the train finally started moving, some air came in through the cracks. It stopped somewhere along the way and stood still for hours in the blazing heat. They eventually arrived at the station in Merksplas, Belgium, near the Dutch border. The inmates were led to the penal colony there, accompanied by swearing German soldiers who were lashing out wildly. When they arrived, they encountered staring people with strange looks on their faces. Pierre quickly realized that these were sick prisoners who belonged in a psychiatric institution. Most of them were insane and extremely dangerous. In the Merksplas prison they were all assigned a number, a prisoner's uniform and a cell. There too, hunger, poor hygiene and oppression were an everyday part of life.

Aalst
Although Pierre was gradually turning his back on his religious

beliefs, Franske and Emilienne lit a candle for him every evening before they went to bed, and they said a prayer for him with their father.

Jef rang the bell. Franske ran to the door to let in his uncle. Emilienne offered him a stool so he could join the group – some Resistance fighters from the Great War were already visiting. Celina poured the coffee and Pa Florent passed around the cigar box. He talked about his visit to his son in St Gilles prison.

'Pierre wasn't allowed to take the cookies we'd brought for him,' said Franske.

'They're nothing but cruel thugs,' bellowed one of the men, furious.

'Do you have any news of our Pierre?' Pa Florent asked his brother, while he was lighting his cigar.

'Maria, my wife, heard they sent him to Merksplas, a transit camp. Where he'll go from there is anyone's guess!'

It grew silent at the table. One of the Resistance fighters broke in and said that Mussolini had been deposed after the Allied landing in Sicily. General Dwight Eisenhower, the Commander in Chief of the Allied forces, had announced the Italian capitulation.

'Maybe so, but Mussolini is still in power in northern Italy, thanks to the support of the Germans. But the new Italian regime has chosen the side of the Allies,' Pa Florent responded.

Celina poured some more coffee, and when it ran out she left for town to buy more.

The situation for the citizens of Aalst had deteriorated. The price of food had gone up, and on the black market the cost of necessities had gone sky-high, butter and bacon especially so. Some farmers were cleverly profiteering by bending the rules regarding livestock, and sold meat on the black market for an extortionate price. No wonder people were stealing on a massive scale: they were hungry.

'Didn't the Germans promise to increase the bread rations?' Jef asked.

'Those were just empty promises. Last night, in retaliation, the houses of some German-loving Aalst families were covered in swastikas,' said the man sitting beside Pa Florent.

Jef suddenly felt very uneasy and left. He felt tormented by the idea that he hadn't had time to patch things up with Pierre after their argument. It was eating him up. He tried to keep his emotions under control, but it was no use. He burst into tears and rushed home.

Merkplas, Belgium

The Germans were strutting back and forth pompously in the Merkplas prison. The guards' constant whispering was making the prisoners nervous.

The following morning, there was an unusual amount of activity in the corridor. Cells were unlocked, and Pierre and a few of his peers had their possessions handed back to them. They quickly put on their clothes. While they were waiting to be picked up by the SS, a newly interned prisoner – one who'd been severely beaten – told them that Mussolini had been liberated by an elite corps of SS officers and was setting up the new Italian Republic on Lake Garda.

One of the guards assembled the prisoners and let slip that they were going to be deported. Sometime before noon, the group was herded like animals into a railcar. A German Army officer intentionally tossed a piece of bread inside after them, causing a kerfuffle when the starving prisoners fought to grab a piece. The train started moving while the SS officers were still shoving the doors closed and locking them. The destination was unknown. The people were being transported in appalling circumstances. The stench was unbearable. Pierre reached out a hand to someone who was about to pass out.

'Keep standing up, otherwise it'll all go wrong!' he said.

The frail girl clutched his hand to have something to hold onto, and gave him a distressed look. Judging from her hand, Pierre could feel she was emaciated. Her eyes were dark brown and her head had been shaved. He tried to use his body to protect her from being crushed by the overcrowding.

'How old are you?' Pierre asked.

'Fifteen!'

'Where are you from, and how did you end up here?'

'I'm Jewish, and I come from Antwerp. One night my parents, my little sister and I were dragged from our beds. I was loaded into a truck and taken away. The Germans locked me up in a dark pen. Today they put me on this train.'

Pierre remembered the newspaper articles in which Hitler openly stated that he wanted to eradicate the Jews.

'I'm Pierre. What's your name?'

'Ella.'

The prisoners were dying of thirst. In the railcar, one man collapsed from the overcrowding and was trampled underfoot by the closely packed prisoners.

GRAZ, AUSTRIA

After a few hours the train stopped, but the doors to the railcar remained bolted shut. In the early evening they could hear barking dogs approaching. Someone beat on the outside of the railcar with a club and the sound sent tremors through the train. Ella almost collapsed from pure terror. Pierre wrapped his arms around her waist right away and held onto her firmly. He whispered: 'Be strong, Ella, we'll get through this!'

Suddenly, the doors of the railcar flew open and the prisoners were driven out with clubs. The young girl grabbed at Pierre's arm with both hands. He pulled her out of the mob and used his body to shield her from the blows. The body of the man who'd been trampled was hoisted onto a wheelbarrow and taken away. The teenagers turned to each other for comfort and support, but then something occurred that should never have happened! Heavily armed Germans herded the prisoners into the courtyard. Ella held tightly onto Pierre's arm. The Germans called out the numbers of the prisoners. Ella let out a shriek when she was separated from Pierre. She was choked with fear, and all the color drained from her face, making the dark circles around her eyes and the cold sores on her lips even more distressingly noticeable. She looked inconsolable. The fifteen-year-old girl suddenly turned around. The German in charge gave her a forceful blow with his club. She fell, her body shrank into a cramped ball and she died on the spot. The German poked her body with a stick, but by then all the life had drained from her.

Ella was loaded onto a wheelbarrow and carted away while the prisoners were held at gunpoint. Pierre hysterically pushed his fellow prisoners aside, trying to force a path to the German who had murdered Ella.

'Don't do it!' Ewald said under his breath.

He held the teenager back. For the first time since his internment, Pierre burst into tears. Ewald tried to comfort him. They were led to the prison, escorted by armed SS guards with dogs on leashes. Pierre's breath caught in his throat when he saw the wheelbarrow containing Ella's lifeless remains pass by. He couldn't stop thinking about the cowardly way Ella's life had been taken from her. He felt demoralized and right then you could have taken away his whole world!

The frenzied dogs on the Germans' leashes were pacing back and forth, pawing the ground impatiently. The glare of the Germans' flashlights was reflected in their eyes. With their growls and bared teeth, the animals warned the prisoners to stay in line and not to try anything funny. The inmates were herded up to the fortress high on the rocks. Once there they were led inside, accompanied by the sound of the Germans' incessant bellowing. They were ordered to take off their clothes and wait. The naked prisoners huddled closely together because it was terribly cold. The gateway was closed and locked.

At the break of day, the gateway was opened again. The German soldiers disinfected the newcomers, using razors to shave their heads, armpits and pubic hair. After that, each prisoner received a number and a work uniform. They were split into groups and led to their section of the fortress. Bunk beds were lined up against the wall, and on each bed was a straw mattress covered in burlap. At the sound of a bell, breakfast was handed out; it consisted of a piece of bread and a mug of some brownish liquid. The exhausted inmates thought they would finally be allowed to rest, but nothing was further from the truth. At the next whistle everyone was made to go outside for roll call, where they were inspected, insulted and spit on.

'You will work until you drop,' said one of the SS guards. Pierre knew that 'extermination through labor' were Hitler's words.

The short speech made the prisoners shudder. They prepared to leave for their appointed workplaces, exhausted to the core. They hadn't slept for days. Pierre was sent to a workshop a few miles away to work with wrought iron, which the prisoners then had to put into position. From time to time they would also be forced to excavate the deep system of tunnels in the granite rock under the fortress on the Schlossberg. Pierre realized he'd ended up in Graz: he knew the historical inner city well, because he'd spent some vacations there with his mother and father. The picturesque city at the foot of the Alps had suddenly become a hell. Even the carillon in Graz's famous Clock Tower had lost its charm.

A sense of trust and a friendly bond quickly grew between Pierre and Ewald, strengthened by their hellish living conditions. Ewald was a German who'd turned against Hitler; he'd been apprehended because he'd saved a Jewish man from the clutches of a German officer. On their way to the workshop where they'd been assigned for the time being, Pierre asked his fellow prisoners if they had any idea where the Germans had taken Ella's body. The inmates shrugged their shoulders, but then one of them said: 'I once had to cart away a dead prisoner.'

'I want to give Ella a decent burial,' explained Pierre.

'That'll never work,' said the fellow, lowering his voice because an SS guard was approaching.

The prisoners arrived at the workshop. Pierre and Ewald were immediately sent to the workstation at the back of the building. It was a confined space, just a few feet square, where some twenty prisoners were working with hammers and blowtorches. Pierre and

Ewald were given some rudimentary instructions and taught how to handle the tools. The noise from the hammers and the heat from the blowtorches – used to turn rods of wrought iron into veritable works of art – was horrific. Once completed, the wrought-iron objects were then hoisted onto the prisoners' backs so they could be carried to the place where they would be installed. At noon the men were given a spoonful of vegetables, a piece meat and a liter of water. It had been a long time since Pierre had eaten any meat.

A few minutes later they were led to a truck that had been parked at the entrance gate; it was loaded with iron bars. Pierre and Ewald were ordered to unload the metal and pile it up. The work was heavy and left them breathless. The young men could hardly lift the bars – they weighed a ton. They didn't have any work gloves and the wrought iron left deep gashes in the palms of their hands. Pierre and Ewald wiped the blood with the sleeves of their work uniforms. After fourteen hours of backbreaking labor, the prisoners returned to camp. The way back was every bit as grueling. Ewald practically collapsed from exhaustion, but Pierre offered his workmate a shoulder to lean on. When they finally arrived at the fortress, they weren't allowed inside immediately. It was below freezing and a harsh north wind was blowing. The prisoners shivered, their lips turned blue and the freezing cold made their hands and feet ache. After a long wait, the warmly dressed German officers finally showed up. The roll call could begin. Pierre and Ewald were told there wouldn't be any bread for them that night because they hadn't managed to unload the truck's entire contents. Ewald stumbled on his way to the barracks. A German officer who happened to be in the vicinity gave him a firm kick and spewed all manner of accusations at him. That evening, all Ewald and Pierre were given was a cup of coffee substitute. One of their fellow prisoners surreptitiously passed them a crust of his bread. A few minutes later, the barracks were bolted and the lights turned off. Pierre went to gather some information from the guy who'd once carted away a body.

The prisoner told him: 'I was made to dump the corpse a few hundred meters from the road we take every day to get to work.'

'Really?' Pierre whispered.

The man explained how he could get there. That night, Pierre tried to formulate a plan, but he was so exhausted he fell asleep.

The lights in the fortress were suddenly switched on at five in the morning. The prisoners only had a few minutes to make their beds, get into their work uniforms, scarf their piece of bread and gulp down their coffee substitute. During that time, Pierre managed to concoct a plan with his buddy.

'Stay close to the route. The SS are everywhere. Be quick and make sure to be back at the workshop on time. Otherwise they'll hang you!' warned his fellow inmate.

Ewald was worried and kept a close eye on Pierre. On their way to work there was a scuffle at the back of the group, which distracted the SS guards. Pierre took advantage of the situation and slipped away. He ran quickly and didn't look back. He arrived at a clearing in the woods and saw the rectangular pit. The earth around it had been scraped away. Pierre crept closer, peered over the edge and shuddered at the site of the decomposing remains. At that moment he realized how fleeting human beauty is. The stench was vile. Pierre held his nose to keep from vomiting. 'I've got to get back,' he thought to himself.

A clicking sound made him look up. Pierre was staring straight into the eyes of a German. Just as the soldier was about to pull the trigger, Ewald strangled him with a piece of wire, making a deep gash. Blood spurted from the soldier's carotid artery. The man crumpled. Ewald dragged the SS soldier to the edge of the pit and shoved him in with his foot. He disappeared into the depths.

'That was a close call! What made you come?'

'I had a bad feeling and followed you. Hurry up – we've got to get back,' whispered Ewald.

They ran to join the others. Pierre couldn't shake off the image of the dead bodies with their mouths gaping and their limbs akimbo. In the distance, they could hear Germans shouting and cursing. They approached the group and saw how the SS officers were spitting on and kicking a prisoner. He was being forced to crawl to the workshop on his hands and knees because he'd started some trouble. Pierre and Ewald rejoined the group unnoticed. The prisoners were counted before they entered the workshop. The numbers added up, and they were allowed inside.

That afternoon, Pierre ran into the prisoner who'd told him how to get to the burial place. 'Well, did you find Ella?' the man sneered. Pierre gave him a hearty shove. The prisoner fell, quickly pulled himself up and hurried away. Pierre took a rod of wrought iron from the rack and returned to his station, where one of the SS men asked Ewald: 'How did you get those blood stains on your clothes?'

Just as Ewald was showing the German the deep gashes in his palms, the sirens started to wail. The prisoners were quickly rounded up and locked in a separate area, while the Germans all rushed to the bomb shelter. The workshop shook from the heavy bombing. A short time later the inmates returned to the fortress. That night, in the skies over Graz, all hell broke loose again. Pierre lay staring into the darkness and listened to the thunderous explosions; they sounded close. 'Too bad I wasn't able to bury Ella,' he said to himself.

Thoughts of death pursued him throughout the night. Pierre relived his mother's death – he could almost see it happening. The boy remembered how his little brother Franske had gone in search of his dead mother. They'd found the toddler, almost three, crying in the attic.

'I can't find Mama anywhere!' the little fellow had cried.

It was a tough night for Pierre.

Aalst

Food shortages were causing a lot of problems in Aalst. A farmer went complaining to the city's mayor about some sacks of grain that had disappeared from his barn. The military police were powerless to do anything. Theft was rampant. As a precaution, Pa Florent had stacked his supply of firewood in the cellar.

Celina was becoming worried because she couldn't get any more coffee on the black market, and Pa Florent drank a lot of coffee, especially now he'd heard that his daughter wasn't living in St Gilles but in Germany, with the son of a German judge. This made Pa Florent furious – he felt his daughter had deceived him. He was also worried about his son's fate. Pierre was constantly on his mind. He couldn't visit his best friend Gaston anymore, because the Germans had also picked him up. Luckily, Pa Florent had a lot of friends willing to offer moral support during this difficult period. When they came to visit, he told them that he'd heard that Berlin was being subjected to days of heavy bombing, and that there was serious fighting taking place on the Eastern front. They also discussed the new Italian Prime Minister Badoglio, who had declared war on Germany. While Celina poured the coffee, Pa Florent said: 'Celina told me there was a raid was on the grounds of the Aalst soccer club. What exactly happened there?'

The man beside him explained: 'The military police surrounded the playing field during the last few minutes of the match. Some supporters ran, shots were fired, and a man and two kids were wounded and taken to hospital. The Germans checked everyone's papers, and they arrested some seventy supporters.' Then the man asked: 'Did you guys hear that the Germans are taking down the bells of St Martin's Church?'

The gathered friends could hardly believe their ears, because last July the Germans had promised – in writing – to leave those bells alone. They went to see for themselves.

Graz

In Graz, one of the German guards was missing. They'd been trying to find him for some time. For over a week the soldier's disappearance had remained a mystery. Search dogs were sent out again to comb the area, but they couldn't find a single trace of the man.

The German officers in charge regularly selected one of the teenage inmates to spend the night with them. Then, in the morning, the German military command would meet with the troops. The boy who'd repeatedly been raped throughout the night was then required by the Germans to serve the coffee. At that particular meeting, the soldiers were asked if anyone had noticed anything suspicious or had any idea where the missing SS guard had last been seen. One German explained that on the day the man went missing, he'd found one of the prisoners with blood on his clothes.

'Did he have an explanation?' The commanding officer asked.

'His hands were bloody and covered with deep gashes from his work with bars of iron.'

Beyond that, nothing much was said. The young boy who'd overheard this discussion passed on the information, in revenge for having been abused.

Some weeks later, there was still no trace of the missing German. Ewald was interrogated once again, but he maintained that the blood on his clothes came from the injuries on his hands. The SS officers didn't believe him, and they locked Ewald in the fortress's cellars. They questioned his friend Pierre, who refused to answer, and so they beat him viciously. That didn't achieve anything: the teenager kept his mouth shut. After the questioning, Pierre was sent to the workshop. He had a dizzy spell in the corridor and stumbled.

'Did you murder that German?' a fellow prisoner asked while helping Pierre up.

'No, I didn't do it!'

'If you did, I would've been more than happy to lend a hand,' answered the prisoner.

Pierre tried to cool his anger on the wrought iron, but the hammer landed on his thumb, and he screamed in pain. The SS guard in charge just chuckled and ordered him to keep working. Pierre developed a splitting headache from the endless droning ring of hammers hitting the iron bars. The prisoners were exposed to a hellish level of noise in the workshop; the Germans all wore earplugs. When he was finished, the boy hoisted the wrought-iron object onto his back and carried it outside. It had had to be carted up the slope to be put into place.

As the prisoners were returning to the fortress, it started snowing. Pierre thought about Ewald as the landscape turned white, but the pain in his blue, swollen thumb absorbed all his attention. One of the prisoners – who happened to be a doctor – looked at the injury and said: 'That fingernail has to go. You ought to go to the sickbay in the fortress later on.'

'Unspeakable things go on in that sickbay. You can hear the prisoners crying and groaning in the middle of the night. I'd rather stay well away from there,' replied Pierre.

That night, the pain in his bruised finger woke him up. Pierre tried to work the nail loose himself, but he fell asleep listening to the rats squealing. Later, a soldier dragged Pierre from his bed – it was his turn to satisfy the Germans' needs. Pierre started trembling, and as he bent over to put on his wooden shoes he spotted the rat poison. He quickly picked up a few grains and swallowed them. The cramps started right away. The Germans pushed the boy along, caressing his back and pinching his buttocks. Pierre felt sick to his stomach. He was shoved into a room full of SS officers, where he immediately felt a drunken German's hands all over him. The poison did its work, and he started vomiting blood. After that, the Germans kicked him outside. He lay on the ground, writhing in pain, and couldn't stop throwing up. Pierre thought he'd die there and then, but once he'd gotten all the poison out of his system he started to feel better. He went smirking to his cell and noticed that his loose fingernail had fallen off.

A week later Ewald was questioned again. Nothing new came to light. The Germans sent him back to the workshop. Pierre felt relieved when he saw his buddy back on the shop floor.

A heavily loaded truck stood parked in front of the factory gate. There was a layer of snow covering the transported goods. Pierre and Ewald were ordered to unload the truck. Ewald's knees buckled a couple of times. The SS guards made sure that the unloading of the wrought-iron bars went smoothly.

That same day, an older man collapsed from the workload. His body was immediately hoisted onto a wheelbarrow and carted from the shop floor. The prisoner who'd taken bodies away before was again enlisted to do the dirty work. It was heavy going, pushing the wheelbarrow through the woods in the snow. The cold north wind blew straight through his thin clothes, and he was blinded by the white snowflakes. The prisoner stopped the wheelbarrow in order to steal the dead man's prison uniform.

'Sorry, chum!' he said while putting the corpse's clothes on under his own.

When he got to the burial pit, he dragged the body from the wheelbarrow.

'Farewell!' the prisoner said, shoving the deceased down the hole.

He looked briefly over the edge of the pit. To his enormous surprise, he noticed that the body had fallen on top of someone in uniform: the impact had shaken some of the snow off of the jacket. The prisoner left the wheelbarrow where it was, ran to the camp, and told the guards what he'd seen. The Germans responded immediately. The prisoner who'd discovered the body was permitted to select another inmate to accompany them. The SS officers leashed their dogs and went to the place where the missing soldier had been found. It was dark in the woods, so they shined their flashlights to show the way. When they arrived at the pit, the Germans remained a safe distance from the edge. They tossed a rope and a flashlight at the prisoners.

'Get that soldier out of the pit!' ordered a German officer, but neither prisoner wanted to go down into the deep hole. The fellow who'd found the missing German was ordered to tackle the job, and tied the rope around his waist at gunpoint. His companion, cursing and gagging, lowered him down. He wiped the snow away with his hands while his buddy held the light from above. The uniformed German quickly appeared. Out of curiosity, one of the SS officers went closer to the pit and stared over the edge.

'That's him!' he said.

They hoisted the prisoner from the pit, together with the dead SS man. Later that night, the body was examined for clues. The wire that had been used to strangle the officer was still stuck in the deep gash, and it carried a maker's mark. That was bad news for Ewald because he was the only one in the workshop with access to that type of wire. They dragged Ewald and his workmate out of bed. Pierre was questioned again, but he let nothing slip. Ewald was cruelly tortured. The two friends stood with their backs against the wall. Just then, one of the senior officers arrived, up in arms. He chewed out the SS officers and took Pierre away from the wall. In the meantime, the guns were loaded.

'Don't do it!' Pierre shouted.

In front of his eyes, Ewald's body was riddled with bullets. Pierre jerked himself free from the guard's grasp and confronted the men who had shot Ewald. He was furious but was quickly overpowered by the SS officers and locked up in a constricted concrete pen less than two feet high. The stench was unbearable. Pierre lay on his stomach. His hands gripped the iron bars through which an icy wind blew. He was disgusted by the grinning smirk on the face of the SS guard walking back and forth nearby. Suddenly, the man turned on him and kicked the iron bars of the pen. Pierre quickly pulled his fingers away. The man drew his index finger along his neck as if he were slicing it with a razor, and walked away. Snowflakes drifted through the air, making everything seem peaceful for a moment. Pierre tried to use his feet to push away the object that was blocking the space, but without success. It felt wet to the touch, but he couldn't see what it was exactly; it was too dark in that oppressive space. An hour later, it stopped snowing. The snow made a creaking sound under the boots of the German who was approaching the enclosure. He put a cup of some steaming beverage in front of the bars, with a piece of bread beside it. When the crunching sound of the SS guard's footsteps died away, Pierre stuck his hand through the bars. Sadly, the food was out of reach.

It was freezing in that pen. Pierre was burning with a fever and soon fell asleep. He became delirious and woke up with a start, imagining he saw Hitler dangling from a noose. The boy started up and bumped his head against the tarred concrete ceiling. In the meantime, the snow reached halfway up the iron bars. He put a handful of snow into his mouth to quench his thirst. When he looked outside, he noticed that the clouds had disappeared. Pierre felt ill. His heart was racing, he was shivering and his teeth were chattering. A little while later, Pierre broke out in a sweat. He heard someone coming and looked outside. Pierre recognized the officer who had saved him from the firing squad. The man passed him some bread, sausage and something warm to drink. Astonished, Pierre reached through the iron bars with both hands.

'Thank you,' whispered the teenager. He accepted the food and immediately crammed it into his mouth. Now that some daylight was starting to shine in, he tried to see what was at his feet, but he still couldn't make it out. The liquid oozing from of the thing stunk horribly and had spread all over the floor of the pen by then. Pierre groped around until he felt stubbles and a head with a gaping mouth. He shrieked, pulled his hand away and realized he hadn't been lying in this pen alone. His entire body knotted up with an indescribable fear. The boy gagged. He wanted to get away but couldn't go anywhere. The pen was so narrow that his limbs were forced to come into contact with the corpse. A sharp pain in his neck took his mind off the horror. He noticed that painful sores were covering his entire body. His fever shot up, and he lost consciousness.

Aalst

Back in Aalst, Uncle Jef saw a man who was ordered to halt on the street; but instead of stopping, the man ran on and was shot. He was taken to the hospital. A few hours later, Jef learned that the man was a prominent member of the French Resistance. Jef went to see his brother to tell him the news, but Pa Florent had already heard all about it from his friends.

Pa Florent picked up the letter he'd received from Eveline. He looked sad because his daughter had let him down by running away with a German.

'She sounds OK. She writes that she doesn't want me to worry. Eveline mailed this letter at the beginning of September, and now it's 30 December 1943. It was exactly one year ago today that Pierre was picked up by the military police. I can still picture his arrest. I'll never forget the words he said. Hopefully, this horrific war will be over soon. Have you been able to find out where Pierre is? The uncertainty is making me sick!'

'No one knows where they've taken him,' answered Jef.

In the meantime, Franske and Gustaaf were bickering. They couldn't agree about how to divvy up the stickers Eveline had tucked into the envelope for them.

'How are things with Gustaaf's health?' Jef asked as he was leaving.

'He still has asthma attacks on a regular basis. I'll let him stay here until New Year's. After that, he's going back to the family that lives near the hospital' Pa Florent said under his breath.

The needles were falling off the Christmas tree that Emilienne had put up much too early. By the morning of New Year's Eve, the branches were almost entirely bare. Emilienne had made garlands out of newspaper to brighten the place up. Pa Florent folded five envelopes, one for each child. He wrote their names on the outside, put in some money, and placed them in one of his inside pockets. Celina went to prepare the New Year's Eve meal. She sharpened the knives to slaughter the turkey they'd been fattening in the garden, tied her apron around her waist and went outside. The pen was empty and the door open. Celina hurried inside and called out: 'Someone stole our turkey!'

'Sacre bleu!' Pa Florent bellowed.

Franske and Gustaaf couldn't believe it and went to see for themselves, but Celina was right: the turkey was gone. Pa Florent sent Celina into town to get something tasty for the kids, but food was scarce on the black market. She bought eggs, flour and sugar to make *oliebollen*, a type of doughnut traditionally eaten in the Low Countries at that time of year.

At the stroke of midnight, following a Belgian tradition, Franske and Gustaaf read their New Year's letters out loud. These letters usually rhymed and contained good wishes directed at the parents. In return, the children were given envelopes with some money. Pa Florent had two envelopes left over – one for Eveline and another for Pierre. He put them away in the drawer of his desk.

The next morning, Uncle Jef came to wish everyone a happy New Year. He gave each of the children some bank notes for their piggy banks. Jef had cigars for Pa Florent and chocolates for Celina. He also had an envelope for Pierre and Eveline. Pa Florent put away the one for Eveline and placed Pierre's envelopes next to his unopened

Christmas present. Jef noticed that Pa Florent had trouble holding back his tears. Celina put the coffee and the rest of the *oliebollen* on the table. Jef couldn't resist *oliebollen*. He sprinkled some extra powdered sugar on top and ate a few more. Then the doorbell rang. 'More visitors,' said Jef as he stood up to leave.

A steady stream of visitors arrived to wish Pa Florent a happy new year. They brought him coffee and chocolate, things that were difficult to obtain. The men started talking about the intensive bombing in Berlin, and about the starvation raging in their districts. In Aalst, the per capita bread rations had been increased slightly, and dried herring and other less desirable types of fish were distributed to keep people from starving. The church council opened a soup kitchen in the parish hall.

A short time later, Uncle Jef turned up at Pa Florent's door with news that three armed Resistance fighters had stormed the hospital in Aalst, commando-style, to free their leader who was recuperating there. They'd disarmed the guard on duty and threatened the hospital staff with their weapons.

'I heard it all revolved around a guy named Scijffert. The Germans accused Agent Lefèvre, the guard whose gun had been taken by the Resistance, of complicity.'

'I know, the Germans always follow the armed Resistance's activities with reprisals. That security guard will no doubt be the next victim,' replied Pa Florent.

After that, Jef said that Eisenhower had been appointed Supreme Commander of the Allied forces. That was something Pa Florent hadn't heard; he must have missed that bulletin. He turned up the volume of the radio.

'You do know that listening to English stations is illegal?'

'Yes, of course, I know that! But what difference does it make? I'm already on the top of the list to be shot.'

The men smoked the Cuban cigars Pa Florent had gotten for New

Year's from an Englishman, who'd been given them in turn by an American pilot. The man was hiding in the cellars of Terlinden Castle. A growing hum made the brothers look outside. A large fleet of American and English planes was flying over Aalst.

'Could a landing be near?'

'That's what people are saying,' answered Pa Florent as he stepped outside.

Graz

In the fortress in Graz, Pierre was taken out of the narrow pen. He was so sick and weak he could hardly walk. Boils were covering his entire body. The swelling in his neck was so prominent that he was sent to the sickbay. Pierre refused to go, so one of the SS officers held a gun to his head, and he went to the doctor under duress. The doctor could see right away what the problem was, and the teenager had to lie down to be treated. The military doctor cut open the pustules with a knife and smeared them with some coal tar ointment he'd made himself; no other medicines were available. Pierre screamed – the pain was excruciating. The doctor needed all his strength to tackle the largest boil in his neck. At that, Pierre blacked out. It was hours before he regained consciousness.

'You can go now, but come back tomorrow,' said the doctor.

'I'm never going back there!' Pierre said to himself.

Back on the shop floor, Pierre hoisted a weighty piece of wrought iron onto his shoulders. The boy grunted and puffed and was ordered outside to install it up the slope. SS guards stood along the side of the road armed with whips and clubs to keep the prisoners in line. The temperature had dropped below zero, and it was snowing. The inmates returned to the fortress late at night and marched past the ramparts with their strongholds and gatehouses. The strategically located medieval fort's other buildings were ideal for locking up and torturing prisoners. The towers gave the

Germans a bird's eye view over the ancient fairy-tale city along the River Mur. Once the prisoners entered the inner courtyard, they were forced to bide their time until roll call. As usual, the officer in charge kept them waiting. The sound of the carillon ringing in the clock tower sent shivers down Pierre's spine. It was bitterly cold high on the mountain, and his hands and feet had gone numb. An hour later, the officer finally showed up for roll call, roaring drunk. The man didn't even check to see if everyone was present – he just kicked and screamed and sent everyone back inside. The freezing prisoners took off their work clothes and washed and shaved without soap, using what little water was available to them. They pulled on their uniforms over their wet skin, because they had no towels to dry themselves. Everything had to happen at top speed because the evening meal was being dished up. The prisoners wolfed down the vegetable mixture. Shortly after that, it was lights out in the dormitories. Ewald's bed had been taken over by a large Italian Mafioso, whose feet dangled over the edge. He snored like a pig and kept everyone awake. According to the Germans, Fernando was a murderer, but Pierre had his doubts: the Italian was constantly in tears.

After a few days, Fernando's true nature emerged. He stopped crying, chewed out a fellow prisoner, bullied the older inmates and almost choked someone to death. Pierre became wary of the mobster. The coffee substitute and bread were handed out at around five o'clock in the morning. The Italian stole a fellow inmate's portion, and a fight broke out. Fernando held the angry man at arm's length with one hand while he stuffed the stolen bread into his mouth with the other. His behavior became increasingly erratic: it almost seemed as if he wasn't right in the head. He was violent one minute, anxious and distraught the next. Everyone avoided him because it was clear there was something wrong with the man. One night, he really kicked up a ruckus. He woke everyone up, shouting and screaming. Fernando was cold and grabbed other peoples' blankets. Another day, the thug had had enough of being hungry. He went over to the provisions shed, battered down the door and stole some food. One of the SS guards grabbed hold of him. But Fernando was strong, very strong, and he flung the German against the wall. Other soldiers immediately rushed to the soldier's aid. It took five people to subdue that bear of a man. The Italian was locked up in a pen, but a short time later he escaped. He was quickly apprehended. Not a soul ever saw Fernando again. Some claimed that the SS officers had murdered him, but there was no evidence.

Pierre noticed that more and more prisoners were pouring into the camp. He was even forced to share his bunk with a stranger who'd been severely beaten by the Germans. The man explained that he'd been accused of assisting an English pilot. While the teenager was helping the man put on his shirt, he carefully asked for news. 'The Americans are carrying out air attacks on Germany. They've bombed Wilhelmshaven to smithereens,' the man whispered.

Pierre smiled. For the first time in a long while, he felt a glimmer of hope, but the situation in the camp was becoming increasingly desperate. Food grew even more scarce. People were becoming sick because of the poor hygiene and overcrowding.

In the middle of the night, Pierre was woken by the sound of the SS guards' hobnail boots marching through the corridor. He jolted awake, and guards dragged him out of bed. He was led outside while the Germans quarreled among themselves. The boy was forced to join other prisoners waiting in the courtyard. It was bitterly cold, and the inmates huddled together to keep from freezing to death. After a long wait, the Germans finally came outside. One of the SS officers read out numbers from a list.

Those who were called had to follow the man to the place where they'd assembled when they'd first arrived at the fortress. There, the prisoners were given back their possessions. Pierre clasped his things close to him and inhaled the distant scent that reminded him of home. He put on his clothes, but they hung so loosely they hardly fit. Then, accompanied by the loud roar of a German escort, they were led to a truck: their destination remained a mystery. The overloaded vehicle came to a halt after a short drive. The Germans, shouting and cursing, herded the bewildered people out of the truck's cargo area. The drunken SS guards kicked and beat everyone in their path. One of the soldiers looked Pierre straight in the eye; the teenager felt disgusted by the man's intrusive gaze and the grin on his face. The prisoners were led to a railway car.

Aalst

In Aalst, the shortage of fuel meant that classrooms were no longer heated. Then the schools were closed because of impending bombing raids. Hundreds of American and English planes were flying over. The tension people were living under could be cut with a knife. To take the children's minds off the situation, Pa Florent showed them his deceased father's album filled with photographs and newspaper clippings.

'Tell us more about your father,' said Franske, who hadn't known his grandfather.

'The newspaper articles speak for themselves,' answered Pa Florent.

But, because Franske and Emilienne insisted, he decided to tell them more. Celina stirred the fire because fuel was scarce and outrageously expensive. She sat down and joined the convivial group.

Pa Florent explained: 'My father was a well-known figure in Aalst. He was very sociable, a devout Christian and he took an active role in city politics. He owned an extensive collection of books about many different topics.'

'Are his books in our library?' Franske asked.

'Most of them are, yes.'

'Papa, tell us more,' Emilienne asked.

'My father was an alderman in Old Aalst. He was on the governing board of the Council of Almshouses. He was committed to helping orphans and was an honorary chairman of the Orphaned Boys' Society. Here is a picture of him being honored by the city of Aalst for his efforts. The National Health Services also gave him a medal. When my father died, his body was laid to rest in his house on the Zoutstraat. In this picture, you can see the people lined up, waiting to pay their last respects. I still miss my father every day.'

The English radio station interrupted the cozy discussion to announce massive air attacks taking place over Germany. Pa Florent held up his palm to shush his children. He put away the family album and spent the rest of the day glued to the radio.

THE CONCENTRATION CAMP IN ROLLWALD, GERMANY

The rumble of planes overhead startled him. Pierre recognized the American aircraft; seeing them gave him a glimmer of hope. He had heard all about the Americans' capabilities from his father. The Germans attacked the enemy with artillery fire.

In the meantime, the prisoners were put on a train to be deported. The temperature was below freezing, and the railcar was unheated. The victimized inmates were crammed into that stinking compartment for fourteen long hours, with nothing to eat or drink. You could see the desperation in their faces. They stared despondently into space, hungry and trembling from the cold. Some of them collapsed from the ordeal and were trampled by the others. The prisoners broke off icicles that had formed inside the railcar and took turns licking them. When the train finally came to a halt, the doors were unbolted. The exhausted prisoners stumbled out into the cold.

'Rodgau-Rollwald,' Pierre read on the sign beside the track.

The SS were waiting for them on the platform, and welcomed the starving group with loud shouting. There were also dogs on leashes, pawing the ground with impatience, waiting to terrorize the defenseless arrivals. The animals had been worked into a frenzy by their handlers and were vicious. Pierre reached out to help a prisoner who had been attacked by a dog. The man had a gaping wound on his calf that was trailing blood. Pierre quickly tore a piece of cloth from his shirt, tied it around the prisoner's leg and helped the man along. The sound of cracking whips ensured the unfortunate prisoners didn't dawdle. A few well-aimed strikes of the whip landed on Pierre, and the marks they left burned the sores already plaguing his pale skin. The trail of prisoners trudged to the heavily guarded camp a few hundred yards away, which was surrounded by high fences. The fence poles were bent inwards at the top and had electrified barbed wire attached to them; between every barrier was a path or a trench filled with water. There were wooden watchtowers spaced at regular intervals, manned by SS guards with machine guns and searchlights.

'This is the beginning of the end,' whispered the man Pierre had been supporting the whole way.

Pierre had once read a book about negativism. He did everything he could to push negative thoughts out of his head, and said to himself: 'Nobody, but nobody knows what the future holds!' He kept repeating that sentence to boost his morale.

A sign hung above the entrance to the camp: 'DAS TOR'. Overwhelmed by fear and suspicion, the prisoners entered the camp. They were immediately surrounded by SS guards and led to a small room in the bunker. The sound of howling and moaning emerged from another one of the chambers. The prisoners soon realized that the bunker was where people were tortured. The Germans had instantly succeeded in terrorizing the new arrivals. The newcomers were each given a number and had to hand over their property. They were disinfected and shaved. Then they were separated into groups and given prison uniforms. The Rollwald camp was divided into a work camp and a concentration camp. Pierre was sent to the concentration camp, where the overcrowded conditions were deplorable. Walking skeletons stared at him, stupefied. They lived in wooden barracks arranged in orderly rows, but a mood of chaos prevailed: the prisoners were insulted and beaten up at the slightest infraction. Pierre was assigned a place to sleep in one of the barracks. Because of the overcrowding, the bunks had to be shared by several prisoners.

The moaning, coughing and rattling of breath kept Pierre awake all night. The next morning the lights came on much earlier than usual, and the SS guards came screaming into the barracks. Pierre jumped up and stood, like the rest, to attention in front of his bunk. The Germans counted and inspected the prisoners. One older man was grabbed and beaten before their eyes because, according to them, he'd been a little slow getting out of bed. The victim howled and shrieked, and he kept sobbing long after the SS guards had left the barracks. The straw mattresses were hastily shaken and neatly arranged. After that, bowls filled with water for washing and shaving were handed out to be shared, one among four people. A short time later the German tyrants came back into the barracks. They shouted and pulled the straw mattresses off the beds because they hadn't been fluffed up enough to suit the guards. One of the SS men noticed that the water the four prisoners had used for washing was still in the bowl. The man closest to the bowl was beaten to a pulp, while the prisoner next to him was forced to drink the filthy water. Once the Germans had left the barracks, breakfast was handed out. Everyone got a piece of bread and a cup of water that was practically undrinkable – it was cloudy and smelled and tasted like camphor.

'In the camp I was in before, they mixed camphor in with the food,' Pierre whispered to the person beside him.

'Here it's only bread and water, with a little vegetable mush now and then.'

Vermin were scuttling in and out of the barracks. A couple of prisoners hunted down a black rat that had tried escape. They quickly caught the animal, tore off its head and took turns sucking its blood. Then they ripped it to pieces and ate it raw. The people in the camp lived under heartbreaking circumstances. Many became sick from malnutrition and poor sanitation. Most of them had chronic diarrhea, pneumonia, and sores all over their bodies.

Even though the temperature was barely creeping above freezing, the concentration camp prisoners were forced to work the land beyond the parameter. An icy wind howled over the fields, but as luck would have it a few rays of sunshine soon poked through the blanket of clouds. The SS guards were waiting for them in the fields. Trucks pulled up all day long, loaded with barrels of fertilizer. Pierre and his fellow inmates had to empty the manure into steel buckets and spread it over the earth. He was startled by the scraping sound of wooden shoes shuffling along the road; the inmates from the adjoining labor camp were filing past. One prisoner, who had been transferred from the work camp to the concentration camp because he hadn't worked hard enough, explained that in the work camp prisoners were given coffee substitute instead of water for breakfast, and potatoes and vegetable mush for dinner, sometimes even a small piece of meat. In the labor camp the regime was less harsh. The inmates were allowed to sleep longer, and at night they knocked off work earlier. The SS guards ordered the concentration camp prisoners to pick up the pace. It was late and getting dark by the time they'd emptied the last barrel of manure. The entire group stunk to high heaven as they returned to the camp, exhausted.

A few weeks later the prisoners were sent to dig the soil in the fields, and they didn't get back to camp for twenty-two hours. In the days that followed, the ground was tilled, raked and prepared for the sowing of potatoes and chard. Just as they were finishing the heavy work and were about to return to camp, a truck pulled up. The female driver got out, and some women with shaved heads sprung from the back of the truck. The driver had long blonde hair and wore a German uniform. She paraded provocatively in front of the concentration camp prisoners. Pierre stared at her and, just for a moment, forgot his woes. Sensual fancies briefly entered the minds of the other prisoners as well. But her bone-chilling snarl at the defenseless women soon chased those ideas from their minds. She shoveled seeds from a barrel and dumped them into the aprons on the women's laps. One of the women accidentally let a corner of her apron slip, and the seeds fell to the ground. Furious, the driver beat her with a steel shovel. The woman's wails caused the prisoners to look back as they were marching away.

Aalst
The schools reopened their doors. The teachers were present, but almost no children turned up because rumors were rife in the Belgian cities about murders, robberies and rape. It was the same story in Aalst and the neighboring villages. People didn't dare go out at night because there was danger lurking everywhere.

There were more and more sirens howling. The English radio stations advised civilians to evacuate the cities and stay away from train stations and power plants. Frightened, Franske and Emilienne crept closer to their sick father, who was awaiting his execution. Pa Florent peeked out the window and saw a squad of German soldiers running through the Parklaan. His face turned white, but the Germans kept running past his house. Pa Florent sighed with relief and turned up the British radio station a little louder, so he wouldn't miss any of the announcements.

Large-scale measures were being taken to prepare for whatever the future might hold. Emergency exits were installed in all public buildings. Some streets and squares were blocked off with iron posts. More bomb shelters were hurriedly being excavated. The Germans were distributing leaflets printed with a mandatory regulation, warning that anyone found helping downed pilots to escape or harboring them was risking the death penalty. The general population was duly notified, but Pa Florent and his friends already had plans in place for assisting Allied pilots in case of emergency.

The unrest in Aalst grew, and the schools were closed again. The sound of anti-aircraft guns was everywhere. The residents who hadn't yet fled the city rushed to the bomb shelters. Pa Florent refused to give in to the violence and remained sitting beside the radio, even though the broadcasts were regularly interrupted; then you couldn't hear anything but static. Franske wanted to remain at his father's side, but he wasn't allowed to. He had to go with Celina to one of the larger bomb shelters in town. Only their dog, Markie, stayed with Pa Florent. Later, bombers appeared in the skies above Aalst. But that day the city was spared. The planes dropped their explosives on Brussels, where there were many casualties.

Celina and the kids were returning home once the danger had passed when they saw some heavily armed gangsters fleeing the National Bank. That very evening, Pa Florent heard news of a failed hold-up there.

The following day, it was Ghent and its environs that were heavily bombed. The explosions could even be heard in Aalst – roughly 100 miles away – and from a few places you could even see the blasts.

Food shortages reached almost fatal proportions, despite the best efforts of the city of Aalst and the church council. Massive plundering of food increased, and those keeping watch were helpless to stop it.

One day, Pa Florent's dog disappeared. Franske and Emilienne went in search of Markie; they combed the entire neighborhood, but they couldn't find the dog anywhere. Franske suspected the Germans of stealing their pet dog, but he had no proof. Behind his father's back, Franske asked every German he encountered if they had seen Markie. The Germans patrolling the city were unapproachable, and they snapped at Franske so viciously that he ran away, scared, and tried going up to some others. Eventually, one of them ordered him to go home.

That night, a neighbor rang the bell. Franske opened the door. The man standing there said he had seen their dog. He described the thief – a single father living with his seven children in a dilapidated house on the outskirts of town. Pa Florent forbade the children to go. But Franske and Emilienne were determined to save their dog. They got up in the middle of the night and slipped out quietly. It was pitch-black: the only light was from the glow of the moon. Now and then they had to evade some Germans who were out on patrol. When they finally reached the run-down house where the single father lived, they peered inside through a slit in the cardboard that was there to replace a window. They couldn't see much, so Franske and Emilienne worked the slit into a bigger hole. Once the opening was big enough to look through, the boy tried again. What he saw chilled him to the bone. Their dog was hanging – head down – from an iron hook, and the father was skinning it. Franske screamed blue murder. Emilienne started running away, dragging her brother with her. As they were fleeing, they looked back briefly and saw the man appear in the doorway, his hands covered in blood. The ruckus had attracted a group of Germans, but the kids leaped over a fence and disappeared into the night. The Germans used their flashlights to search the area, but they couldn't find anything unusual and continued on their patrol.

By then, Celina had noticed that the children were not in their beds. She woke up Pa Florent. He was in a terrible state. When Emilienne finally opened the door at home, she really got it, full force. Pa Florent only calmed down once he realized that Franske was in shock. The children were sobbing, describing what they'd seen. Celina could hardly believe it. 'Sacre bleu!' Pa Florent bellowed. His curse rang through the house. He beat the table with his fist because someone had skinned the family's faithful companion. The children were very upset. Celina sent them to bed, and Franske was allowed to sleep in Emilienne's room that night.

The next morning it was noticeably quiet in the house on the Parklaan, because Markie was gone. It made Pa Florent sad that someone had slaughtered his dog. His English friend had clambered over the concrete fence and come in through the back door. The Englishman was told the sad tale of Markie's fate as soon as he arrived. It touched him deeply – he'd only recently petted the dog. The man tossed back the whiskey Celina had poured him and comforted Pa Florent. The announcer on the English radio station also inadvertently brightened Pa Florent's mood. He said that the Allied invasion of German-occupied Western Europe, led by General Dwight Eisenhower, had begun in the early morning. There had been a spectacular dropping of airborne forces and a massive amphibious attack. They'd stormed the coast at low tide to break through the barricades of the German Atlantic Wall. Then the announcer reported that the German soldiers guarding the beach had surprised the Allies with their violent fanaticism: these young soldiers were prepared to fight to the death for their leader, Hitler. The reporter noted that the landing in Normandy had been a success and that the operation was continuing undiminished.

'Those young German soldiers probably got their combat training in the Hitler Youth. Did you know that the entire Nazi education system focuses on the glorification of the German Reich, the people, and the Führer? Hitler is a god to those German boys,' said the Englishman.

'Here in Belgium, the school systems were reformed to follow the German model. Pro-German figures were appointed to the Ministry of Education. Some schoolbooks were censured, and they were planning to bring in a standardized history book. Jewish teachers were barred from Belgian schools. German inspectors pay surprise visits to classrooms to keep an eye on the lessons. But here in Aalst, the German reforms were held back by the diocese's power over free schooling, which is, for the most part, independent from the government. Up until now, not much has changed in education,' said Pa Florent.

A few days later, Pa Florent read that King Leopold III had been deported – first to Germany, and then to Austria – shortly after the invasion of Normandy. After that he showed his brother Jef, who was next to him, a headline printed in huge type, announcing that Rome had fallen into Allied hands. Jef read the article over his brother's shoulder.

Since the Normandy landing, a steady stream of Resistance fighters had been coming and going from the house on the Parklaan. To avoid attracting attention, they crept over the garden fence and came in through the back. Pa Florent assembled the Resistance fighters' information, in preparation for the arrival of the Allies. There was a possibility that one of the Allied airdrops had been intercepted by the Germans, because Pa Florent heard that only one airdrop has been found in Aalst.

During the second week of September, Uncle Jef told his brother that Belgium's Pierlot government had returned from exile, but for Pa Florent that was old news. Franske ran into the living room waving a three-colored Belgian flag he'd gotten in the city during the celebration of Aalst's liberation. He told his father that people were having a party in town and were handing out ribbons decorated with the colors of the Belgian flag. While Franske was pinning one of the ribbons to his father's shirt, he also said that collaborators were being arrested. Women who'd befriended the occupying forces were being forced onto their knees in the streets while their hair was cut off.

'The houses of traitors are being covered in graffiti; some are even being torn down,' Franske added.

That reignited the argument with Uncle Jef, who'd been sympathetic towards the Nazis throughout the war. Pa Florent hurled blame at him, and Uncle Jef immediately went on the defensive. He hollered: 'Why do you think they haven't shot you yet?'

That made Pa Florent so angry that he grabbed anything in reach and threw it at Jef. As Jef was leaving he shouted: 'Don't forget I did everything I could to save Pierre's life! I even kept the Germans from executing him on the spot.'

He slammed the door of the house on the Parklaan with a bang and hurried home. Along the way, his attention was drawn to the high-speed American vehicles racing through the city. He paused a moment to watch – it was a hive of activity. A fellow resident of Aalst came up to him and said that Brussels had been liberated, and other cities would soon follow. Jef wasn't in the mood for a chat, so he tipped his hat and continued on his way. When he got to his street, Jef could see that the display window of his fur shop had been pelted with eggs. He did an about-turn, made a slight detour and jumped over the garden gate, which was locked, and went in through the back door. That night, Jef's wife washed the word 'Nazi' off the plate-glass and scrubbed the sidewalk in front of the store. She could hear cannon fire in the distance and realized that the war wasn't over yet. They kept the shop closed during the days that followed because Jef and Maria were afraid of being beaten up.

A couple of days later, Jef turned up at Pa Florent's door again. Celina let him in. Jef related how, on the night of the liberation, the celebratory mood evaporated when people heard cannon fire in the distance. The residents of Aalst were afraid the violence would flare up again.

'You know, a German convoy drove into Aalst that night. Luckily, the military vehicles made a quick U-turn. That same night the British set up posts by the bridges and access roads to keep them from coming back.'

Pa Florent was surprised to hear it. He turned the radio a little louder as the British announcer sounded the all-clear after England had been hit by a barrage of flying bombs. The report also repeated the news that the Belgian government, led by Hubert Pierlot, had returned to Brussels from London.

King Leopold III was still in captivity. The Belgian government hadn't agreed with his capitulation in 1940, and they'd kept a firm hold on the reins since then. Now that most of the country had been liberated, the government was returning, and Leopold III's brother was to be appointed Regent of the Kingdom of Belgium. Prince Charles swore a constitutional oath on 21 September 1944.

That month, American and British armies, assisted by troops from Belgium and elsewhere, drove the Germans from much of the country. Shortages of food, however, remained a problem; essential items were almost impossible to obtain. Butter, meat and coal were being sold on the black market for extortionate prices. To curtail the use of black-market currency, the Gutt Operation began in October 1944. This restructuring aimed to limit the supply of money and stabilize prices. Bank notes had to be exchanged, their circulation was restricted, and bank deposits, periodic accounts and current accounts were all blocked. There was a run on the banks because this entire operation had to take place within five days.

Signs bearing the names of well-known war heroes replaced some of the city's more familiar street signs. This annoyed Jef. After he'd exchanged his bank notes, he went to his brother's to blow off steam. As soon as Pa Florent opened the door, the brothers started talking about the street signs. As he came through the door, Jef said that Hitler's outstanding general, Erwin Rommel, had committed suicide.

'I'd heard he was the only one who dared to talk back to Hitler, so maybe he was assassinated.'

'No details have been released yet. You know they've stopped printing papers because of the shortages,' Jef replied as he sat down at the table.

'D'you think Pierre is still alive?' Florent suddenly blurted out.

Jef knew that Hitler's war wasn't just about conquest, but destruction, and he answered: 'I have no idea – I don't have any contact with the Germans anymore.'

At that, Florent frowned and looked at his brother dubiously.

'I mean it!' was Jef's response.

Celina just managed to keep the brothers from getting into another squabble. She poured them some more coffee and talked about the jubilant welcome given to the entire municipal government on the town square. Celina went on to say that she'd heard in town that General Eisenhower had issued an order requiring all the Resistance movements to turn in their weapons.

'A lot of Resistance fighters haven't complied because they're afraid the violence will start up again,' Pa Florent countered.

When they'd finished their coffee, Jef left to go home.

The Concentration Camp

Harvest time arrived, and the prisoners were sent back to the fields to dig up the potatoes. Some of the prisoners were hungry enough to forget the Germans were watching them, and they started eating the potatoes right away, but the guards beat anyone caught eating the crop. One of the emaciated inmates didn't survive the thrashing and died on the spot. Pierre was sent from the fields to bury him.

Towards evening, they loaded the harvest onto a truck, and the guards searched the prisoners' pockets before they returned to the camp. Severe punishment was waiting for anyone who'd ignored the ban on stealing.

The suffering in the overcrowded concentration camp became heart-rending. Another day passed during which they had nothing to eat or drink. The prisoners were growing visibly weaker. Pierre knew he had to do something to keep from starving. He didn't lose heart because he'd again spotted American and British fighter planes in the skies overhead.

Pierre and one of his buddies took a risk and crept into the bushes when they were on their way to the place where they were meant to dig a drainage ditch. They quickly grabbed as many acorns as they could off the ground and stuffed their pockets. A fellow prisoner was keeping the SS guards distracted, so they were able to rejoin the group without attracting attention. They divided the acorns among themselves.

There was a wood stove burning in the barracks; winter was coming. The small heater wasn't enough to keep the large space warm, but the prisoners could use it to roast their acorns. The SS guards picked up the scent and wondered how the prisoners had gotten hold of the acorns, but they left well alone. To the Germans' amusement, once the prisoners had eaten the acorns, their stomachs swelled up and they got terrible cramps.

The living conditions in the camp became increasingly horrific. The region was being heavily bombarded, and food supplies dwindled. All these hardships made Pierre and his friend decide to try gathering more acorns. But the Nazis were keeping a close watch along the route to the place where the prisoners had to dig the ditches. The two friends slipped away and crept towards the oak trees. While they were gathering acorns, Pierre heard someone approaching. He warned his buddy and hid. The instant his friend turned to see where the sound was coming from, a bullet hit him in the chest. The mortally wounded fellow made an effort to get away. The Germans came closer, and one of them used his foot to turn the man around so he could put another bullet through his head. Pierre remained motionless until the SS men had disappeared from view. Only then did he dare crawl towards his friend; he closed his eyes and covered his body with fallen leaves. Pierre thought about Ella and said to himself: 'I'm sorry Ella, but I didn't have a chance to bury you.'

Pierre's fellow prisoners were surprised to see him because they'd heard two gunshots. Once again, the prisoners created a distraction so Pierre could rejoin the group. He whispered that they'd murdered his friend. Death didn't frighten the prisoners anymore because they'd become so accustomed to people being killed. Pierre divvied up the few acorns he'd managed to find.

On their return to the barracks that night they each got a cup of water left over from cooking vegetables. The prisoners roasted the acorns on the wood stove to keep themselves from dying of starvation. And, after eating the acorns, they were all sick again. Around five o'clock in the morning, the SS guards stormed into the barracks, roaring. They'd smelled the roasting acorns, and woke up all the prisoners abruptly. Shivering from the cold, the defenseless victims stood to attention in front of their bunks. The oldest, who was responsible for the whole group, was taken away by the SS guards. A little later, the man's bloodcurdling screams could be heard coming from the bunker. His terrifying cries continued until after midnight. The next morning they put the man's mutilated body on display. Shortly after that, it started snowing heavily. It was the harshest winter in years. The snow piled up, and the cold north wind howled through the barracks. The prisoners were suffering terribly, and the hardships and cold were taking their toll. You could see the helplessness in their eyes; it looked as if the connection between their bodies and their souls had been severed.

Aalst

Now that Belgium had been – for the most part – liberated, Hitler was determined to turn the tide by firing a massive number of V1 and V2 bombs, first on Britain, then on Belgium and France.

Jef was on his way home when he was startled by the horrific racket of a V1 bomb flying overhead. He covered his ears while his eyes followed the device. A muted crash soon followed and, in the direction of the nearby town of Mere, a flash of light lit up the sky. Jef was so scared he started running.

The Battle of the Bulge raged on unabated, while V-1 flying bombs, also known as buzz bombs, were ravaging the cities. Bad weather had grounded the Allied air forces, and Hitler was using that to press his advantage, but as soon as the weather cleared the Allies rallied. Around Christmas, the US Air Force bombed the Belgian towns of Malmedy and St Vith. The courageous resistance offered by American troops in St Vith and Bastogne hampered the German Army's advances.

The Battle of the Bulge was over by the end of January 1944, and the Germans were forced to withdraw. Early in February euphoria erupted on the Parklaan when they heard on the radio that Belgium had been completely liberated. Another news item followed, reporting that Soviet troops in Poland had rescued captives held at Auschwitz, the German extermination camp.

Pa Florent's English friend visited, and Celina uncorked a bottle of wine. While they were drinking, Florent's friend explained that Montgomery had led the British Army over the Rhine at Wesel, and a few days later the Americans and the Brits had surrounded the Ruhr district in Germany. The two friends felt certain the Germans would never manage to win the war against the Allied powers. The US Air Force and Royal Air Force were both bombing Germany relentlessly. On the Eastern front, the brutal Russian Commander Zhukov was driving the Red Army with an iron fist, pushing back the German Wehrmacht's combined defenses. As Celina was refilling their glasses, the men discussed the death of the American President, Franklin Delano Roosevelt, on 16 April 1945. Celina turned up the radio: the English station was reporting that the Americans had liberated the concentration camp in Buchenwald, and the Canadians had liberated Camp Erika near the Dutch city of Ommen. When they heard that news, they all cheered. Pa Florent offered the Englishman a cigar, and while the man was helping himself from the proffered wooden box he tried to find out about Pierre: 'Which camp is your son in?'

'He was transferred to Germany, but sadly I have no idea exactly where he is or how he's doing. I think about him day and night. I don't know if he's still alive, or if I'll ever see him again.'

'Chin up, man! The end of the war is near.'

Someone rang the doorbell, so the Englishman tossed back the rest of the wine and slipped out through the back door.

Gustaaf leaned on the bell until Celina finally let him in. Pa Florent's face brightened as soon as he saw his son. The boy asked about Pierre first thing.

'I'm sad to say I don't know anything about your brother. But I do know that the Nazi empire has sustained a crushing blow.'

Franske rushed down the stairs when he heard that Gustaaf was back home.

The Concentration Camp

Bombs again rained down on Germany, and new prisoners flooded into the concentration camp shortly after that. To boost the morale of the despondent detainees, one of the newcomers told them that the Americans had captured the – undamaged – bridge over the Rhine at Remagen, and that they had taken over the German city of Cologne. The news made Pierre's heart beat a little faster. Most of the prisoners – even those who had given up hope and just stared into space – were nevertheless briefly heartened by the news.

A large, blond SS man appeared in the doorway of the barracks. He immediately looked towards Pierre. The boy had previously noticed the steely blue gaze of that German watching him. Pierre ignored the look and quickly put on the jacket of his prisoner's uniform, getting in line to go outside for roll call.

The blond SS man came back into the barracks after roll call. His gaze slid over the heads of the prisoners until his eyes found Pierre. The SS officer crept behind Pierre and pulled him towards him. He pressed his body against Pierre's back and ran his trembling hands over the boy's body. Pierre shuddered and felt sick. He quickly took a step forward. The officer grabbed him by the neck and pulled him back again. Pierre jabbed him with his elbow, yanked free and spit in the German's face. Just then, the SS man's superior officer arrived in the barracks. He called the soldier away, who left, muttering under his breath.

There was the sound of terrifying howls coming from the bunker where victims were being subjected to all sorts of atrocities at the hands of the SS. Pierre's thoughts turned to all the injustices the prisoners were forced to endure. He still had no regrets about resisting the occupation in Belgium, because he had no wish to live in a dictatorship; he wanted to live in a country that made freedom possible. The SS intended to make him pay for going against Hitler's will. The boy had suffered immensely and realized he'd had enough. He had decided to fight off the German officer's unwelcome pawing. Nasty images kept him awake all night. When the lights went on in the morning, the boy had hardly slept. Pierre and his fellow prisoners jumped up, shook their straw mattresses and folded their blankets. They wormed into their filthy clothes without washing, because the pipes had frozen. Pierre wiped the congealed blood off his feet, which were covered in sores from scraping against his wooden shoes. Then he hurried outside with his fellow prisoners for roll call. The hellish noise of the bombers dropping their explosives near the camp made the Germans race for cover. 'They're American and English bombers,' Pierre said to himself with glee.

While the prisoners waited in the yard, paralyzed with fright, Pierre noticed a smoldering cigarette that one of the Germans had hastily tossed on the ground. Everyone in the camp was longing for the taste of tobacco, but nobody dared break ranks. Pierre didn't hesitate: he went to the burning cigarette, picked it up off the ground and took a sizable drag. Then he passed it on to his fellow prisoners. To the inmates, every inhalation was pure pleasure. Some even had tears in their eyes.

The American-led bombing raids didn't let up. The city of Rodgau was severely damaged, and the Rollwald concentration camp, a mile or so to the south, was shaken to its core. More and more Germans were losing faith in the regime. Some SS guards, left in charge of the overcrowded camp, fled. But a hard core of the SS stayed on to continue terrorizing the prisoners until the bitter end. After Pierre had been beaten and yelled at for no apparent reason, he was measured. The SS officer he'd rebuffed pushed a shovel into his hands, so he could dig his own grave outside the camp's walls.

An incident unfolded just as he and some others, all destined for the same fate, were about to leave the camp. The Germans marched together into the yard, shouting. One of them held a list in his hand. Another was restraining a child who was being kicked and beaten. There was some discussion among the SS – they all kept looking at the list. They placed a noose around the child's neck, at which the boy started reciting verses from the Torah. The Germans were infuriated. They tried to silence the child using any sadistic means possible. But the boy didn't stop. He was hoisted up and hanged. The SS men watched expectantly, but the Jewish boy was putting up a fight. Then the Germans ordered one of the prisoners to hang from the child's legs. But that didn't do any good, so the boy was cut down and wrestled to the ground. Then the SS men kicked him around like a rubber ball. While all this was happening, the Jewish child emitted a bloodcurdling cry. Although Pierre opposed violence with all his heart, his body was too weak to follow any orders from his brain, and the Jewish boy suffered a horrific death. The condemned prisoners, struck dumb by the atrocity they'd just witnessed, left through the gates of Camp Rollwald, shovels in hand. Pierre took one final look at the concentration camp where he'd suffered so terribly, and went to his death, exhausted.

A mile or so from camp, the guards used a stick to draw lines in the sandy ground, to show Pierre where he had to dig his own grave. The Germans ordered him to get started. When they had indicated the location of all the graves, and the rest of the prisoners had set to work, the SS kept driving back and forth. Sometimes they stopped to mistreat one of the condemned men, and if their victim collapsed they ordered someone else to bury him. Then the Germans drove off again.

THE LIBERATION

When the condemned prisoners had finished digging, they heard the rattle of distant motors; the jeeps were coming in their direction.

'Now we're finished!' Pierre said aloud, at which point the prisoner beside him burst into tears.

Pierre turned to look, but he couldn't see a single sneer, or any sign of hate, on the face of the camouflaged soldier. The man approached, passed Pierre a cigarette, and spoke the words of deliverance: 'I'm an American!' The boy's sense of relief was immense. There are no words to describe what he felt at that moment.

From there, things went very fast. The prisoners were hoisted onto the vehicle and they raced off, coming under German fire along the way. It was all happening so quickly that Pierre only grasped how narrowly he'd escaped death once he'd arrived – safe and sound – in the American camp. The prisoners were at a loss to show their gratitude to the Americans. Pierre harbored tender feelings about the heroic deeds of the American soldiers who'd risked their lives to save him. The weakened boy pulled a few strands of thread from his prisoner's uniform and gave them to the man who'd come to his rescue. The American placed the strands in his leather wallet, next to a picture of his girl. The rescued prisoners were given first aid, and then they were transported in military vehicles and handed over to the Belgian Army.

Aalst

Two days later, on 30 April 1945, a military vehicle came to a halt on the Parklaan. Pierre got out of the jeep, supported by military personnel. The neighbors hurried outside to get a look at the boy, who was severely undernourished. Franske opened the door; he didn't recognize his brother right away and was even a little frightened of this walking bag of bones.

'Franske, it's me!'

Franske recognized his brother's voice and hollered: 'Pierre's back!' Emilienne was the first to respond to the hubbub. She was upset. Pierre offered her a piece of chewing gum he'd gotten from his rescuers, and Emilienne popped it in her mouth.

'Sacre bleu! Our Pierre has come home!' crowed a euphoric Pa Florent when he saw his son.

Pierre had completely forgotten that the Great War had left his father so scarred; the reality came as a shock. Pa Florent phoned the doctor. Celina was speechless when the emaciated boy turned up in the kitchen. Gustaaf had been about to leave for the hospital, and he walked – amazed – to the car that had been sent to pick him up.

Franske and Emilienne raced to Uncle Jef's to share the news, and he came to the house on the Parklaan right away. There he wrapped his arms around his nephew and cried. The boy had lost a lot of weight in the concentration camp. The family doctor had meanwhile arrived. He examined Pierre and diagnosed a lung infection and a weakened heart. Then he changed the ointment and sterile bandages the Americans had put on Pierre's festering sores. He asked the boy a few questions, but Pierre was in no condition to put his thoughts, feelings and story into words. He showed no emotion. The doctor sent him to bed.

'Pierre may have survived his stay in the camps, but he will remain scarred for the rest of his life. It will take him a long time to recover. Try not to ask him too many questions,' whispered the doctor to Pa Florent.

Pierre had to stay in bed until he built up some strength because his heart had become very weak, but news quickly spread that he'd had returned from the concentration camp in one piece.

Pa Florent's friends came to visit Pierre, bringing along a stack of newspapers. The one on top dated from early May 1945, with Stalin's picture on the front page and the headline: 'The scoundrel is finished!' and 'The Russians take control of the Reichstag.' The friends didn't stay long in Pierre's room because he was too weak to enjoy all the attention. Celina had made coffee, and the men sat around the table downstairs. They were still talking about General Eisenhower, General Montgomery and Admiral Bertram Ramsay, and about the spectacular Normandy landing, which had taken place on 6 June 1944. They also discussed the liberation of France and the Battle for Paris that had ended on 25 August 1944, when Paris was finally freed. Then Pa Florent added: 'It was on Midway that the fighting spirit of the Japanese was broken. That was a turning point in the war. After that, the Japanese were defeated on Guadalcanal. If the Americans had lost on Midway, then the United States wouldn't have had enough resources to protect the West Coast, and the landing on Normandy might never have taken place.'

Pa Florent's friends exchanged glances – they hadn't given it much thought, but they realized there was a kernel of truth in his way of looking at things. Celina closed the living-room door and reminded the men to lower their voices. A short time later the friends went home, and silence again descended on the house.

Pa Florent became worried because his son didn't show any emotion at all, not even when he heard that Hitler had committed suicide. When Franske went into Pierre's room to tell him that Montgomery had accepted the capitulation of all the German armed forces, Pierre just stared vacantly into space.

Towards the end of May, Pierre asked about his sister, Eveline. His father told him the whole story: that Eveline had run off with a German officer shortly after Pierre's arrest.

'She lives in Germany and has a two-month-old daughter. I've broken off all contact with her. I've since heard that her husband committed suicide, just like Hitler.'

Pierre kept staring at the ceiling and showed no emotion. Luckily, Franske was there to cheer things up. He brought his brother the newspaper every day and placed it on top of the pile on Pierre's bedside table. Then he'd hop onto the bed and tell Pierre everything that had happened at school. Pierre wasn't strong enough to read himself, so Franske offered to read him the paper, but their father wouldn't allow it. He sent Franske downstairs.

'Papa, whenever I close my eyes I'm back in the middle of all that horror.'

'Try not to underestimate the impact of what you've endured. But don't keep the memories of that time of suffering locked up in your heart.'

Pa Florent realized that his son's experiences had left deep scars, so he got into his wheelchair and went out to look for a suitable present for him. He rode all over town until he finally saw what he was looking for in the window of a small shop.

When he got back home, he went straight to Pierre's room. The boy ripped open the package and smiled for the first time since his return. He put the American flag his father had given him on the bedside table. Pa Florent switched on the light at the base of the flag and said: 'Looking at that little flag will help you let go of all the feelings you're bottling up. Here, I'm putting a pen and a notebook next to it. When you feel ready, write something: it's important to start at the beginning. The words will help you re-live the events. The memories of what you've been through will never go away, but I'm sure that once you've gotten your thoughts in order, the chaos in your head will disappear.' Then his father left the room.

Every time the boy remembered the horrors of the camps, or thought he heard people crying, he looked at that flag and heard in his head that soldier's words of freedom saying: 'I'm an American!'

At the end of August 1945, Pierre was staring at the new notebook beside his bed. He reminded himself of what had happened with his previous *cahiers*. He picked up the notebook and ran his fingers over it. Then Pierre put it back on the nightstand and picked up his pen. It had been a long time since he'd held an object like that in his hands. Then he put down the pen. He glanced at one of the headlines on the front page of the newspaper and drifted away in thought.

One day, Pa Florent came into Pierre's room and noticed that the stack of papers had shifted. Pa Florent sat down on the bed beside his son, and told him about the glorious summer weather and the flowers that were blooming in the garden. When he got back downstairs, he whispered to Celina, overjoyed: 'Things are picking up with Pierre.'

Within a month, Pierre was reading all the newspapers stacked up beside his bed, and a short time later even started to read books again. It was another six months before he'd built up enough strength to leave his bed and get back on track. For the rest of his life, whenever it was quiet, he could hear that soldier's words of freedom: 'I'm an American!'

END

About the author

Belgian author Vera Mertens made her debut in 2015 with Nakato, *followed in 2016 by* The Mystery of Göteborg. *She then realized the time had come to put her father's war experiences on paper, so the younger generation could learn from his ordeal. The result is* The Concentration Camp: The True Story of a Belgian Teenager. *She is currently working on a book about the dangerous world in which we live today.*

Pierre grows up in a family still scarred by the Great War. When the Second World War breaks out, the Germans invade Belgium. Pierre's yearning for freedom and justice drives him to join the Resistance to fight the occupying enemy. On 30 December 1942, the German Gestapo apprehend him at home and the teenage boy ends up in a German concentration camp, where he is subjected on a daily basis to the horrors taking place. He never loses heart, because American and English airplanes regularly appear in the skies overhead.

CPSIA information can be obtained
at www.ICGtesting.com
Printed in the USA
LVHW080059121122
732937LV00004B/835

9 781528 915434